AROUND PORTLAND WITH KIDS

JUDI SIEWERT DAVIS   KATHRYN WEIT

DEDICATION

This book is dedicated to our family and friends
for all their assistance, patience, and understanding.

1993 Edition
Printed in Oregon
Published by Discovery Press
P.O. Box 80366
Portland, Oregon 97280

ISBN: 0-9614261-3-6
Editor: Dianne Sichel
Photography: Judi Siewert Davis
Research: Louise Davis

CONTENTS

INTRODUCTION

When people ask how to entertain children, suggestions tend to be the old favorites like the Zoo and OMSI. These attractions, of course are not to be missed, but there is more, much more, in the Portland metropolitan area. In **Around Portland with Kids**, we give you ideas on what to do and where to go. Ideas we have explored, researched, and sampled firsthand. Hopefully, our book will stimulate your curiosity, as it did ours, to discover Portland and the metropolitan area, whether it's with a guide or on an adventure of your own.

The Excursions and activities are designed for children and adults to do together. This is not only for safety, but also to give adults and children an opportunity to enjoy and share an adventure together. To help make your experiences more enjoyable, we've included a list of suggestions.

• Have a day pack for explorations, ready and waiting. This will eliminate last minute searches. Items to Pack:

—Several plastic bags for carrying first-aid supplies (band-aids and cotton balls sprayed with antiseptic); extra bags for treasures, tissues and trash.

—A map of the city for directions and to mark with colored stickers the places you have visited.

—Binoculars for finding wildlife, or searching out landmarks from viewpoints.

• Call ahead for current information on hours, costs, and any special requirements for handicap access. We have tried to be accurate, but changes occur. Those places that charged admission at the time of publication are indicated by this symbol. $

• To preserve memories, don't forget to bring a camera (with film!) and flash when appropriate.

• Make a habit of bringing along small notebooks and pencils for keeping a journal of discoveries.

• Return to sites to observe the changes of time and season.

• Many of the places in this book are on or near private property. Please be considerate, stay on trails and be responsible for your own litter.

• Always let someone know where you are going and when you expect to return.

We welcome any comments, suggestions or additions you might wish to make. Write us at Discovery Press, P.O. Box 80366, Portland, Ore. 97280.

Macleay Park

WALKS

Portland is a walker's paradise. Only minutes away from downtown, you can take a sidewalk stroll along the river or a deep woods hike.

We often hear parents complain that their children don't like to take walks. Halfway through what started out as a wonderful family outing, they find themselves carrying a whining child.

There are a number of things you can think about and prepare ahead for even for the simplest walk that will improve the chances for success.

Remember that a walk with a child will not be exercise for you. You must walk slowly and explore the little things. Peek in the hole in the tree, tickle the earthworm, throw stones in the stream, touch the moss, wonder at the beauty of trees. Children should not be allowed to walk too far ahead - side trails can be dangerous. If you're taking a city walk, make time to stop for an ice cream or window-shop.

Consider the age, endurance, and interests of your child. We have included in this guide a variety of walking locations, lengths, and levels of difficulty.

Don't forget the packs we recommend at the beginning of the book. Bring along high-energy snacks and something to drink. Add a magnifying glass. Consider physical comfort items such as sunglasses, bug repellent, and sun screen.

Walking can be a stimulating physical and mental activity that in the Portland area can be enjoyed outdoors, rain or shine!

Leif Erikson Road

Leif Erikson Road was once the main road through Forest Park. Now closed to vehicular traffic, it is a favorite of walkers and joggers year round. During summer, temperature always seems to be at least 10 degrees cooler here than in the city. On a warm, wet, winter day you can hear the background sounds of water dripping off the trees and watch the fog ooze down the hillside.

If you have the time and inclination, you can hike over 7 miles on Leif Erikson Road. The roadway intersects the ubiquitous Wildwood Trail (the main Hoyt Arboretum/Forest Park Hiking Trails) in many places, and it is possible to take walks deeper into Forest Park. If you want something much shorter, there are also rewards. Between the 1/4 and 1/2 mile marker there is a turnout with a spectacular view of Mount Hood, Mount St. Helens, the Fremont Bridge, Port of Portland, and Portland's east side. Another viewpoint is just beyond the 1/2 mile marker.

Note: Trail is a paved in places dirt/gravel road with a gradual incline. Good for beginning as well as experienced hikers. Roadway has distance markers.

Directions: Follow NW Thurman to the very end where it becomes a dirt road. Park the car along the roadside when you come to the gate. Hike begins here.

Glendoveer Fitness Course

This is a two-mile trail around the Glendoveer Golf Course. It is well-maintained and popular. The special treat for children are the wild/domestic bunnies that inhabit the wooded areas that the trail passes through. If you do not want to do the full 2 miles, begin to the left of the parking lot and double back when tired. There are also rabbits in the wooded area to the right of the parking lot.

Directions: Enter on 148th Street between NE Glisan and Halsey. There is a public parking area and the Fitness Course is clearly marked. Dogs are not allowed.

Bridge Walk
Circle tour across Hawthorne Bridge, Eastside Esplanade, Morrison Bridge and Tom McCall Waterfront Park.

Portland is a city of many bridges, but we seldom take the time to enjoy them by foot. This tour offers a closeup look at two of Portland's bridges plus unique views of the city and waterfront. When you walk the bridges, look up and down the river to see the different types and uses of the bridges crossing the Willamette River. There are 10 separate bridges crossing a 10 miles stretch of waterway. Notice the styles of opening and closing. Some are vertical lift others swing lift.

Note: Because of secluded areas included in this outing, we strongly recommend that the walk be done in a small group. We also suggest that you avoid peak traffic hours when bridge traffic is fast and furious. Despite the drawbacks, this is an adventure walk that should not be missed.

Directions: Park on west side near the Hawthorne Bridge. Take the stairs on north side of bridge, staying on the north sidewalk. Crossing the bridge, note the Eastside Esplanade and fire station directly northeast. This is where you're heading. At the east end of the bridge, take stairs going down. Walk through parking lots to the fire station. Sometimes the fireboat is moored here. The Esplanade entrance is directly north of the firehouse at Third and Main. Take Esplanade to winding ramp leading to Morrison Bridge. Walk up the ramp and across the bridge using the south sidewalk. At the end of the bridge head down the ramp at Front Avenue. Take the stairs under the street to Tom McCall Waterfront Park and continue along the seawall south back to the Hawthorne Bridge.

Macleay Park-Balch Canyon
Entrance to Lower Macleay Trail at NW 30th and Upshur

The Balch Canyon/Lower Macleay trail is rated tops for beginning hikers. The trail winds through deep forest along rushing Balch stream. There are wooden bridges to cross, waterfalls, and mossy pools. Hike here year round, but because there are so many deciduous trees it is particularly beautiful in the autumn. The trail connects with the Wildwood Trail and can be followed into Macleay Park on NW Cornell Road. After a little over a mile, you will find a moss-covered stone house. A great place to tell a fairy tale.

Directions: Entrance to Lower Macleay Trail at NW 30 and Upshur.

Portland Audubon Society/Pittock Bird Sanctuary
Wildlife Care Center
5151 NW Cornell Road Portland, 292-6855
Hours: Daily, 10-4pm.

Start your hike with a stop at Audubon House. Here you will find information about trails, wildlife, and Audubon activities. Audubon House has an extensive bookstore focusing on the Northwest outdoors.

The Wildlife Care Center (open 10-3, 292-0304) is designed to care for injured and abandoned wild animals. You can see some of the permanent residents, as well as learn about the care of wild animals.

There are several trails, about .6 of a mile each, which wind through woods and meadows.

Note: Good for beginning hikers and an excellent place to bring binoculars for bird watching.

Directions: Take NW Lovejoy west to Cornell Road.

Oaks Bottom Wildlife Refuge
Below Sellwood Park at SE Seventh and Miller

Oaks Bottom Wildlife Refuge is 110 acres of river bottom habitat on the east side of the Willamette River. It is one of the choice wildlife habitats within the Portland city limits and a favorite for bird watchers. We saw several heron and ducks in one short morning stroll. This is a good walk for people of almost any age.

Note: Great for bird watching and small wildlife, so be sure to bring binoculars.

Directions: Begin hike at northwest end of Sellwood Park near parking lot. A marked trail meanders down the hill through the woods. At the base of the hill, bear right into the wildlife refuge.

The Eastside Esplanade
Runs along the eastside of the Willamette River, from the Hawthorne Bridge to the Burnside Bridge

This walk has a marvelous view of the downtown skyline and Portland's bridges that we usually see only fleetingly as we rush by in speeding cars. The walk is particularly pleasant in the Spring when azaleas planted along the Esplanade are in full bloom.

Note: Because of the secluded location of the Esplanade, we strongly recommend that this walk only be done with a small group. Although the walkway is wide, there are steep drops to the water in places. The freeway is immediately to the right on the other side of a chain-linked fence. The walkway is flat, paved, and accessible to wheelchairs and strollers.

Directions: Take Water Street, turn toward the river onto SE Main. Park at the end of the street. The fire station is on the left, entrance to the Esplanade is to the right.

Hoyt Arboretum
4000 SW Fairview Blvd.
Portland, 228-8732

The 200-plus acre Hoyt Arboretum contains a collection of more than 650 species of trees and shrubs from all over the world and has the largest grouping of conifers in the world. This lush park, five minutes from city center, has more than 10 miles of trails and meadows, including a paved trail with wheelchair access. A great spot to hike and picnic.

A sampling of the trails are:

• Redwood Trail: Begins by shelter, circles and ends by shelter. Mainly conifers, this trail is usually shady on a hot day and also offers more protection on rainy days. The trail is approximately 1 mile. Wheelchair and stroller access possible.

• Oak Trail: Begins and ends by Tree House. Primarily deciduous trees, this is a good place to see flowering trees in the spring.

• Bristlecone Pine: Paved level trail, designed for handicapped access. To get to the trail, turn left off Fairview on to Fischer Lane. The parking lot on left is the start of the trail. Approximately 1/4 mile long.

These three trails have self-guided tour books that can be obtained for a small fee at the Tree House. The Wildwood Trail also winds through the Arboretum. Arboretum staff also provide guided tours for children. Call for information.

Directions: Follow directions from Washington Park Zoo. When you come to Fairview, turn right. Park at shelter. The Tree House, the visitors' center offering trail guides and information, is across the street.

Forest Park-Wildwood Trail

Forest Park is 4,700 acres, 8 miles long and 1 1/2 miles wide, in the northwest hills of Portland. It contains more than 50 miles of trails. The park extends from Burnside Street on the south, to Newberry Road on the north; from St. Helens Road on the east to Skyline on the west. There are numerous points of access.

Maps of Forest Park are available at many locations, including the Portland Visitors Center at 26 SW Salmon, Audubon House, and Hoyt Arboretum. The map contains a trail log (distances) from point to point, side trail lengths, and a profile of the Wildwood Trail. This map also shows areas of direct auto access.

Here are three sections of the Wildwood Trail particularly good for children. You can make these walks either up and back when small legs wear out, or two car shuttle hikes. Since there are many points of access to the Wildwood Trail, look at a map before selecting your rendezvous point.

• Japanese Garden: Walk or ride truck from the entrance of the Japanese Garden on SW Knight up hill to garden. Trail is outside garden and follows ledge above. It is possible to look down into parts of the garden.

• Pittock Mansion: 3229 NW Pittock Dr. See signs for Pittock Mansion on W Burnside. Trail begins at Pittock Mansion, in the northwest corner of parking lot. Trail goes down wooded hillside and can be quite steep in places.

• World Forestry Center to Arboretum: Trail begins behind the World Forestry Center and goes through the Arboretum.

Lewis & Clark College
615 SW Palatine Hill Road
Portland, 244-6161

This is a walk around the grounds of the old Frank estate, which is the heart of the Lewis and Clark campus. The grounds are laid out in large grassy tiers. There are two stone gazebos, small ponds with fountains, and a reflecting pool that is great for sailing toy boats. Below the reflecting pool is a swimming pool which is open to the public. Near the pool are two beautiful grape arbors: a comfortable place to cool off on a hot day. Further down the hillside is a large and well maintained rose garden. On a clear day, there is a beautiful view of Mt. Hood. This is a great outing for families with young children. There is a fitness trail in the woods below the estate.

Note: It is best to do this excursion when the college is not in session or on weekends, as parking is often a problem.

Directions: I-5 to Terwilliger exit. Turn left off Terwilliger to Palatine Hill Road and enter the campus at Gate 3. Continue past the sports center, bearing to the left, take the cobblestone road down the hill past the library. Take the first right. There is a sign for the rose garden and picnic area.

Crystal Springs Creek
Reed College Campus
SE 28th, one block north of Woodstock

This walk explores the headwaters of Crystal Springs Creek. From SE 28th, turn onto the Reed College Campus, at Botsford Drive, and park by the theater. The entrance to the campus here is just down and across the road from the Crystal Springs Rhododendron Garden. Walk up the roadway toward the Reed College swimming pool and you will see Reed Lake, usually full of hungry ducks. Follow the trail around the pond. When you come to the bridge, you can either go across or walk a little further into the marsh area. The marsh is the origin of Crystal Springs Creek. There are lots of birds and frogs.

To continue the walk, backtrack and cross the bridge, following the trail the rest of the way around the pond. You will see where the stream leaves the pond and you can follow it a short distance past the swimming pool, through the field. Here the stream is only a few feet wide and rapidly moving. You can take a small foot bridge across the steam and come up the theater stairs to your car.

Crystal Springs Creek continues, flowing through the Rhododendron Garden, Westmoreland Park, and Johnson Creek Park, where it becomes a part of Johnson Creek.
(See PARKS)

Oregon City Promenade
Located in the upper part of historic Oregon City

The Promenade runs along a windy bluff overlooking the Willamette River in Oregon City, once capital of Oregon Territory.

Walking south from the elevator, you will have a bird's eye view of Publisher's Paper. The Willamette Falls are spectacular from here and you get a sense of the awe original settlers must have felt. Heading north, the Promenade goes a short distance to stairs that will take you under Singer Hill Street, through a tunnel, to the McLoughlin House Museum and other historic houses. Continue down the stairs alongside cascading pools of water, known as Singer Falls, to the foot of the bluff.

Note: Elevator is free. Good place for binoculars. Good for strollers and wheelchairs.

Directions: Park your car near the Oregon City Municipal Elevator at the corner of Seventh and Railroad Avenue. Take elevator up to Promenade.

See MUSEUMS and RIDES for other activities in Oregon City.

John Inskeep Environmental Learning Center
19600 S. Molalla Ave.
Oregon City, (Clackamas Community College)
Hours: Daily, 9am-dusk. Pavilion Open Tues-Sat.

The John Inskeep Environmental Learning Center is a 3 1/2 acre landscaped area at Clackamas Community College. It features native trees, shrubs and plants selected for their attractive appearance and ability to provide food and habitat for native birds and animals. Many of the rabbits and ducks living here are quite friendly.

The pavilion has displays related to wildlife and the environment. Nearby is a full scale recycling center. There are no dogs allowed.

Directions: Oregon City exit from I-205. Follow signs to 213 and Clackamas Community College. Once on campus follow Douglas Loop north.

Tualatin Hills Nature Trail
East of SW 170th, North of TV Hwy. and west of Milliken Way

This 180-acre undeveloped wilderness area is located in the midst of apartment complexes and business parks in Beaverton. While the park is still in the planning process, there are many enjoyable trails for family outings. Since changes are planned, the Tualatin Hills Park and Recreation staff request that you call for current information on trails and parking.

McCarthy Park/Freightliner Walkway
Swan Island

McCarthy Park is a tiny, little used, pocket park on Swan Island that offers access to the river's edge for rock throwing, toe dangling, or watching commercial river traffic. Adjacent to the park, the Freightliner company has developed a scenic walkway along the bluff overlooking the beach. A wide, paved pathway with benches, lights, and seasonal flowers makes this a great place for a beginning cyclist, strollers or wheelchairs. You'll find it quiet and away from city traffic noises. It is a good spot to watch the river tugs and the loading and unloading of ships across the river.
Directions: Take 1-5 north to Swan Island exit. Take Channel Avenue and watch for the sign for McCarthy Park near the "Ports of Call" office complex. Park and walk to water's edge.

Jantzen Beach

A short, paved walkway overlooking the Columbia River offering great views of houseboats, river traffic, swans and ducks. It's in the flight path of Portland International Airport, so the airplanes fly low overhead.
Note: This is a pleasant, easy walk for beginning hikers.
Directions: Jantzen Beach exit off 1-5. Park near Jantzen Beach Bowling Lanes at the south end of Jantzen Beach Shopping Mall.

Walk toward water and turn right. The walk begins about 1/2 block from Jantzen Beach Lanes, opposite Building A. Past ramp 6, the walkway makes a half circle, ending behind the Toys R' Us store.

Marquam Nature Trail
Portland, 228-8732 (Arboretum)

The Marquam Nature Trail winds through the deeply forested Marquam Ravine only minutes from downtown Portland. There are several ways to hike the trail. We have included two.

Council Crest to Marquam Nature Park Orientation Center on SW Sam Jackson Parkway

The Marquam Trail goes through a deep wooded canyon and along a forest stream for a part of the way. The total hike from Council Crest to the Marquam shelter is 2.5 miles, downhill. This hike is best done using a two car shuttle system. The hike begins just below Council Crest Park. Look for a sign along the edge of the wooded hillside facing east that indicates the Marquam Trail.

To prevent getting sidetracked, stay on the most heavily traveled trail. At several points you will see other trails, but these lead to private residences. Where the trail splits, take a left going downhill. Continue down this trail to the Marquam Nature Park Orientation Center on Sam Jackson Parkway. From here the Carnival Restaurant, an old favorite of Portland families, is just .1 mile to the left, down Sam Jackson Parkway.

Note: The trail is for average to good hikers. The trail crosses roads at several points and the section of the hike between Greenway and Fairmont is short and level, an excellent trail for very young hikers. Since at each street crossing the trail is clearly marked, sections may be taken as separate walks.

Loop Trail

A slightly shorter loop hike begins and ends at the Marquam

Nature Park Orientation Center. From the Center walk up a dirt road marked by two metal posts. This section of the hike, approximately 1/4 mile, climbs steeply. When you come to the wooden steps bear right, up the steps. You will eventually come to a split in the trail. Take the Sam Jackson Trail that branches to the right. (The Marquam Trail will continue straight, to Council Crest.) The Sam Jackson Trail will loop back to the parking lot at the Orientation Center.

RESOURCES

"50 Hiking Trails
Portland and Northwest Oregon"
Don and Roberta Lowe

"The Portland Walkbook"
Peggy Robinson (Out of print. Available in libraries, and perhaps used book stores.)

"Forest Park and Forty-Mile Loop Hiking Maps"
Available from Portland Park Bureau

"A Pedestrian's Portland"
Karen and Terry Whitehill

"Portland: An Informal History and Guide"
Terence O'Donnell and Thomas Vaughan

"Portland Step-by-Step"
Joe Bianco

See DAY TRIPS for additional hikes and EXCURSIONS for neighborhood walks.

EXCURSIONS

These adventures are designed for adults to share with children. We hope these experiences will help your children to better understand and enjoy the community, and perhaps, the world, they live in. The people involved with these activities are open to visits. We ask, however, that even though some of the excursions are designed to be less formal and even spontaneous, that you be sensitive to the interests, age, and size of your group. Please be aware of busy days and hours of the place you visit and enter and leave with little disturbance.

We hope that you will be inspired by some of our ideas to discover your own adventures in the area.

MUNICIPAL EXCURSIONS

City Council
1220 SW Fifth
Portland, 823-4000

City Hall is the place to see our city government in action. City Council meetings take place on the second floor, every Wednesday, at 9:30am, and again at 2pm until adjournment. Meetings are open to the public. For a council agenda, call 823-4086. If time permits, you may be able to visit the mayor's office; call ahead for a visit - 823-4120

Multnomah County Commission
County Court House
1021 SW 4th,
Portland, 248-3511

The Board of County Commissioners oversee a broad range

of programs that affect all the citizens of Multnomah County, from animal control to human services and corrections. Meetings are held every Thursday at 9:30, and are open to the public.

Pioneer Courthouse and U.S. Post Office
Between Fifth, Sixth, Morrison, and Yamhill
Portland

Built in 1875, this building is the oldest municipal building in the city. The dark woodwork, brass light fixtures, and fancy elevator provide a sharp contrast to the Portland Building. In the hallway between the post office and the federal offices are many old photographs of early Portland. The Federal Court of Appeals is housed here and the courtrooms are open to the public.

The cupola located on top of the building can be visited, with permission from the guard. (see VIEWS)

Courts

Courtrooms are open to the public. The telephone directory lists locations and telephone numbers of the State Circuit and District courts in the tri-county area.

Fire Station

Visit your neighborhood fire station. For information call 248-0203, and ask the public education officer about visits to a fire station.

Portland Building
1150 SW Fifth
Portland

Most of the city bureaus are located in this architecturally distinctive building. There is a visual arts gallery on the second floor with changing exhibits. Room C contains a wooden replica of the

Portland Fire Station

downtown area, built to scale — a must see before or after a city tour. And, of course, you can't miss "Portlandia" above the entrance on 5th. She is 36 feet tall, made of copper, and weighs 6 1/2 tons !

Police Precincts
4735 E Burnside (East), 823-2143
7214 N. Philadelphia (North), 823-2120

Ask for the crime prevention officer at each precinct and they will help with your visit. See the officers' lockers, patrol cars, and equipment.

Post Office

Visit your neighborhood post office. If you call ahead you may get a tour behind the scenes. Ask for the station manager. Never call in December. For a tour of the Central Post Office (see TOURS.)

GARBAGE TOUR

The Metro area throws out more than 1,700 tons of garbage each day. Ever wonder where it all ends up? Local haulers arrive weekly to dump your garbage into their trucks and haul it off to be squeezed, crushed, and punched tightly together by a powerful automatic compressor. In its much reduced state, your garbage ends up at either the Metro Central Station, located in Portland at 6161 NW 61st (226-6161), or the Metro South Station at 2001 Washington Street in Oregon city (657-7947). Both facilities will be glad to give you and your group a tour.

At both stations the garbage is even more tightly compressed. Next it is packed into large bins and loaded onto gigantic semi-trucks that travel to the Columbia Ridge Landfill in Arlington, Oregon. Daily over 65 trucks make the trip.

Officials say that more than 30% of the garbage we throw out could be recycled. Both stations have marked bins into which the public and haulers can place recyclable materials, including bins for toxic waste. Hopefully, the new curbside recycling service will help in limiting the number of trips to Arlington. For more information on recycling call 224-5555 or Metro Solid Waste 221-1646.

WATER TOUR

The city of Portland and surrounding metro area gets its water from the Bull Run Watershed, located on the Sandy River near Dodge Park. The watershed is a protected area of more than 600 square miles of forest lands. Water is collected and stored in several large lakes (reservoirs) within the watershed area. From the lakes, the water flows through a screen house where it is injected with chlorine and ammonia before the long trip to Portland.

From the watershed, water is carried, by gravity, underground in large conduits. Around 162nd Avenue and Powell, the water is diverted to several locations. Some of it goes to the Powell Butte storage facility; some is sold and piped to other water companies; and the remaining water is carried to the three reservoirs on Mt. Tabor.

The Mt. Tabor reservoirs serve the east side of the metro area. From Mt. Tabor, water travels underground in a westerly direction, again in conduits, to two reservoirs in Washington Park.These reservoirs serve Portland's west side. From reservoirs on the east and west side, water enters the city's water lines, bringing it to our homes and businesses. You might point out to your child the water meter at your home, and then show them the water bill. How many gallons does your family use a day? The Portland-Metro area uses 160 million gallons a day!

FROM WATER TO SEWAGE TO WATER AGAIN

Young children often ask, "Where does the stuff that we put down the drains and toilets go?" The stuff (sewage) goes out from drains and toilets into city sewer collection pipes under our streets. It then flows by gravity to various trunks throughout the metro area, most of it ending at the Columbia Boulevard Sewage Treatment Plant at 5001 N. Columbia Blvd, which, incidentally, is the largest sewage sludge composting plant in the country, possible in the world. More than 831 million pounds of sewage (99.5% water) flows daily through primary and secondary treatment programs. The primary treatment breaks up all solid materials by the use of settling tanks and skimmers. At the secondary treatment stage, micro-organisms are introduced to help remove pollutants. In the final stage, chlorine is added, and the water flows out into the Columbia River.

The treatment of sewage has two recyclable benefits; gas and compost. During removal of pollutants, methane gas is produced, which goes to heat the plant. The gas is also sold to private companies. To make compost, the treatment plant refines undissolved sludge into a refined dry material which is then sold to a composting company. There it is mixed with sawdust and sold as compost to the public to be used in yards and gardens. For tours of the plant call 823-2400.

OLD PORTLAND

There are many ways to explore downtown Portland. You will find some possibilities listed in various sections of this book. We have suggested art tours, museums, and interesting shops and buildings. A whole other approach to getting to know our city involves learning about the past in order to understand and appreciate the present. In downtown Portland, children can see a wonderful juxtaposition of past and present.

We have included bits of historical trivia for you to share with your children as you explore our city's history more fully. Most important, we hope this will aid children to appreciate and develop a concern for the preservation of our links to the past.

Start your exploration by looking at a map of downtown Portland. Notice the angle of the streets as they cross Burnside. Streets south of SW Ankeny were laid out on Magnetic North. In 1845, streets north of Ankeny were laid out by sea Captain John Couch on true North and the North Star. There is about a 20 degree difference between the true North and Magnetic North.

Notice that downtown blocks are small and there are no alleys. The blocks were specifically laid out this way to provide for more corner lots, which were commercially more valuable. Without alleys, deliveries have to be made at the street level, and thus the elevator entrances in the sidewalks.

As you wander around the city, encourage children to develop the habit of looking at the tops of buildings. The real personality of older buildings is often above the ground floor. It is particularly fun to look for carvings of faces, gargoyles and animals. Often the carvings have symbolic meanings. For example, a lion's head means courage, a woman might represent liberty, and a pineapple hospitality.

As you drive along SW Front Avenue, between Ash and Oak Streets, notice the black holes by the windows at the backs of the buildings. These were for hinges for heavy steel shutters that were closed at night to help protect the buildings in case a neighboring building caught fire. Large sections of downtown Portland burned in 1872-73.

Electricity did not come to Portland until 1889. It may be interesting to ask children to imagine living without electricity - how our lives and surroundings would be different. You can see some of these differences in the buildings downtown. Without electricity there were no elevators, so buildings were no taller than three stories. (Additional floors were added after electricity.) The New Market Theater, 1213 SW Ash, was the tallest building in town in 1872.

Large windows were necessary before electricity for both light and ventilation. Compare the building on the southwest corner of Third and Oak with the new Portland Building. Many buildings also were built with open areas in the center. This was designed to provide both natural light and air to the interior sections of the buildings. It was often the location for outhouses!

Notice the buildings with wide doorways and arches. While merely decorative now, these were originally designed to allow horses and wagons to enter. Farm wagons drove right into the New Market Theater building.

Portland has the largest number of cast-iron buildings still in existence west of the Mississippi. More and more of these buildings are being carefully renovated. Take a magnet along to discover which pillars are real cast iron and which are non-metal copies made during restoration. A good area for this test is NW First, from Ankeny to Oak.

Prior to paving, the streets of Portland were dirt and with our rainy climate, mostly mud. Wooden planks were put down to keep the wagons from sinking into the mud. Later, paving stones were used. You can see these stones along the light-rail track and on surface streets around the Skidmore Fountain and under the Lovejoy ramp of the Broadway Bridge.

In many residential sections of town, as well as downtown, the corner curbs still have the metal rim that protected them from being broken down by wagon wheels. The rings embedded in the curbs around town were originally designed as tethers for horses.

Looking across Tom McCall Waterfront Park, it is difficult to imagine the bustling, rowdy waterfront that was once old Portland. In the 1890s, there would have been dozens of masted ships and schooners from all over the world moored at Portland wharfs. (See MUSEUMS, Oregon Maritime Museum.)

Today, we still have many interesting reminders of our seafaring heritage. When the large sailing ships came to Portland, they were often loaded with ballast (rocks and sand) which they dumped when they picked up cargo. There are a number of buildings in the downtown area whose foundations are built from this ballast. One example is the basement level of the Yamhill Market, 110 SW Yamhill. Here you can see an exposed irregular stone foundation wall built from ballast brought in by the masted sailing ships.

Another reminder of those days are the tunnels that run from buildings along Front, First, and Second Streets to the water's edge. The tunnels were used to transport merchandise from the ships to the stores and warehouses lining the waterfront. They were also used for less legal activities such as to shanghai seamen and as opium dens !

The Elephant and Castle Building (1886), 201 SW Washington, has five tunnels leading to the harbor wall. The Bishop's House (1879), 223 SW Stark, has a tunnel that ends at the harbor wall and a tunnel that ends at the old police station at SW Second and Oak. The tunnels are unsafe now and most of them have been bricked up. There are no tunnels open to the public.

Before dams controlled the river level, Portland was subject to periodic floods. The Hazeltine Building at 133 SW Pine has markers that show water levels during the floods of 1892 and 1948.

Special Interest

• Dekum Building(1892), Third and Washington.
Notice that all the entrances to the building are different. There are 308 faces carved around and above the doorways.
• Le Panier, 71 SW Second.
Look for the grinning faces above the doorway.
• Guild Theater Building, at Alder, between Sixth and Seventh.
There are busts of famous composers along the outside of the building.
• New Market Theater, 213 SW Ash.
Count the chimneys! At one time there were stoves for each of the farmer's market stalls. The present chimneys are not functional.

Look at the display on the upper level. It has information about the early days of the building and some artifacts found during restoration .

See the stencils along the first floor ceiling. One is an original from which the others were copied. Can you find it?

Note the size of the doors. Wide enough for a farm wagon to drive through!

Use a magnet on the pillars. Some are original cast iron, others copies.

OTHER DOWNTOWN ADVENTURES

Willamette Center/ MAX/ Pioneer Place

This is a favorite downtown Portland excursion for those dismal rainy weekends. Begin at Willamette Center at First and Salmon.

Upstairs, the Willamette Center is a great place to let off steam. Pretend you're on a space station. Play tag or count the cars as they go under the sky bridge. On weekends the area is deserted. There are tables for indoor picnics.

If you didn't bring your lunch, you can take a short, free ride on MAX to Pioneer Place, where you'll find a food hall in the lower level that dishes up something for everyone's taste and budget.

Saturday Market
Below the Burnside Bridge, off Front Avenue
Hours: Weekends, April - December, 9-5pm, 222-6072.

It is uncertain whether more people go to Saturday Market to eat or to shop. Both can be an almost overwhelming experience. Entering its 19th year, Saturday Market has maintained its tradition of featuring quality crafts and delicious food at reasonable prices. The same craftspeople are not there every weekend, and there are frequently mimes or musicians performing, so every visit can be a unique experience.

Willamette Center

See also DAY TRIPS, ARTS,MUSEUMS, and TOURS

URBAN NEIGHBORHOODS

One of the things that makes Portland a livable city is its urban neighborhoods. Many were originally villages with their own central business districts and school systems and then gradually became a part of Portland as populations grew and city limits expanded.

Unable, or unwilling, to compete with shopping centers and large department stores, some of these areas have cultivated small specialty shops and restaurants while retaining the flavor of the original village. We have included those areas that seem to offer the most to see and do for children and adults. As you walk around, visualize these neighborhoods when they were small villages with wooden sidewalks and unpaved (usually muddy) streets, connected to Portland by ferry or streetcar.

Sellwood

Sellwood was named for the Rev. John Sellwood, who settled the area in 1856. It was incorporated as a village in 1887. A furniture company and lumber mills were its major industries. Sellwood was connected with the communities of Portland, East Portland, and Albina by a ferry that operated from the end of Spokane Street. Streetcars connected it to Portland in 1892, and it quickly became the main junction with the then inter-urban car lines and the electric railroad to Oregon City. See the old stone car barns, built in 1905, at 8856 SE 13th.

The area on SE 13th, between Ochoco and Tacoma, is the old commercial section, now known for its antique shops. Southeast 13th, between Umatilla and Miller, makes the most interesting walking though there are shops scattered all along 13th.

Places to see in Sellwood are: The oldest building (1885-1887) at 1326 SE Tenino; Oaks Park; Oaks Bottom; and Sellwood Park. (See the INDEX for more information.)

St. Johns

St. Johns was one of the first river towns on the Willamette. James John filed the plat in Oregon City in 1852. For a period of time, St. Johns was a part of the city of Albina. In separating from Albina, it became an incorporated village. In 1915, St. Johns joined Portland. Despite its long association with Portland, its geographic isolation on a peninsula between the Willamette and Columbia rivers has helped it maintain a very separate identity.

Redevelopment projects in the downtown area of St. Johns have helped create a lovely small square. The St. Johns City Hall and the St. Johns Bridge are National Historic Landmarks. Worth further exploration are the St. Johns Bridge, Pier Park and Cathedral Park. (See INDEX for more information).

Multnomah

The Multnomah neighborhood is an example of a community that grew as a result of the railroad connections with Portland.

The area was originally settled in 1852, and up to 1890 it was mostly heavily wooded farmland, with the beginnings of a dairy industry. The Oregon Electric Railway Co., which reached Multnomah in 1907, placed the village 15 minutes from downtown. Between 1907-17, the area experienced tremendous growth. The commercial district of Multnomah retains some of the flavor of a friendly rural village. As in Sellwood, Multnomah has many antique and curio shops.

Hawthorne Boulevard

Originally known as "U Street", Hawthorne Boulevard was

named "Asylum Avenue", after the Oregon Hospital for the Insane located on what is now SE 10th and Salmon. When the State Hospital moved to Salem in 1883, the name was considered inappropriate, and the street was renamed in honor of the founder of the institution, Dr. J.C. Hawthorne.

Present-day Hawthorne Street, between about SE 34th and 39th, has developed into an interesting and diverse commercial district. There are antique stores, book stores, restaurants, and bakeries.

Northwest

While several of the other neighborhoods we mention convey the sense of a small town, Northwest 21st and 23rd Avenues, between Burnside and Thurman, are urban in spirit. There are more brick apartment buildings here than elsewhere in Portland and the population is the densest. Northwest Portland has a diversity of people and style found in large city neighborhoods.

There are numerous small specialty shops and restaurants along both 21st and 23rd Streets.

Northwest is one of Portland's oldest residential areas, with buildings dating back to Captain John Couch, who claimed the area in 1885. One example still standing is the small wood frame building at 2061 NW Hoyt. This was originally built as a school for the Couch children and their neighbors. Many of the large old neighborhood homes have been, or are being, renovated. Stroll down NW Hoyt at 17th Street and see the beautifully restored Victorians.

RiverPlace/ Tom McCall Waterfront Park

From atop the Marquam Bridge, Riverplace looks like a small European village in the midst of the city. It is one of the newest additions to Portland's neighborhoods. The development of restaurants, shops, condos, a hotel and marina is located right on the river's edge.

On summer evenings the sidewalks are crowded with people strolling, window shopping, or eating at the sidewalk tables. There are bicycle drawn carriages. Wander down to the piers and look at the many yachts moored here. The piers extend far out into the river at almost water level so you can look up at the the bridges. The walkway continues past the Alexis hotel and connects to Tom McCall/Waterfront Park. You can now walk almost the entire downtown waterfront.

Directions: To get to Riverplace take Front Avenue south to the signs for I-5 south and Riverplace. Parking can be a problem, particularly on weekend evenings. It is sometimes best to park on a side street, walk to Waterfront Park, and follow the walkway to Riverplace.

AIRPORTS

Aircraft At Your Call
Hillsboro Airport, 231-5000

You can see a variety of aircraft, from small planes to corporate jets. Group tours are available from June - August only. For a visit to the tower, call 648-5880 before coming.

Hillsboro Helicopter
Hillsboro Airport, 648-2831

Another airport operated by the Port of Portland. Home of the radio Skyview Traffic Watch, which monitors traffic flow throughout the day. This is a good place to view small airport operations. Helicopter rides are available for children two years and older. Saturday is the best day to visit.

AAR- Western Skyways
Troutdale, 665-0108
Hours: Weekdays, 8-5pm. Group tours available with two weeks notice.

This is a small airport and a part of the Port of Portland Airport system. Visit the flight office, the propeller shop, and see the repairing and washing of planes. It is possible to arrange for a group discount on an airplane ride.

LIVE AUDIENCE TV

The Ramblin' Rod Show
KPTV, Channel 12
735 SW 20th Place,243-2130

A live-audience kiddie cartoon show and a special treat for a birthday person. Call during the first three to five working days of the month to make reservations for the following month. Must call between 10 and 11am. Children must be 3 years and older.

AM/NW Show
KATU, Channel 2
2153 NE Sandy Blvd.,231-4610

A local morning talk show with national and local guests. No children under 6. Must call ahead to get tickets.

MISCELLANEOUS

Oregon Convention Center
777 NE Martin Luther King, Jr. Blvd., 235-7575
Hours: Open Daily, Call To Set Up Group Tours.

The twin glass-and-steel spires rise like a goal-post on Portland's skyline, visually connecting the eastside to the city's westside. The convention center, with its own MAX stop, is jam-packed with art works. There are lobby paintings, hand-painted tile wall panels, a dragon boat suspended from the ceiling, and below the north tower, a giant pendulum swings with the Earth's gravity across a halo of suspended light. Outside are Oriental temple bells and wind bells mounted in clusters of trees.

Clackamas Fish Hatchery
Estacada, 630-7210

The fish hatchery is open daily, 7:30 - 4:30, year round. Summer and spring are the best times to see spring Chinook Salmon. After October, only fingerlings (babies) are left. There are two rearing ponds and other ponds for adult fish.
Note: Call ahead if you bring a large group.
Directions: Out of Estacada, take Hwy.224 and follow signs to McIver Park, on the Clackamas River.

U-Pick Farms

There are more than 75 farms in the area that have either u-pick or ready pick produce. Call the Oregon State University Extension Service (254-1500) for an up to date, free copy of the Tri-County Fresh Food Guide. Be certain to call ahead to check whether children are allowed in the fields.

Storybook Rockery
Rt. 6, Hillsboro
Hours: Daily, 628-1575. Call ahead.

A path goes to the back of this private home where you'll find detailed houses, castles, and characters in their story book settings. All of the buildings are made of stone with small signs in front of each. During spring and summer, ground coverings are in bloom around the area giving the place an added charm.
Directions: Seven miles west of Beaverton on Farmington Road. Look for the white house on the right. If you come to River Road and the Twin Oaks Tavern, you've gone passed it.

Lone Fir Cemetery
Between SE Morrison, Stark, 20th and 26th Streets
Portland, 248-3622 (Pioneer Cemeteries)
Hours: Weekdays, 8 - 4pm.

A walk through Portland's oldest cemetery offers a view of both the good and the tragic in Portland history. You will find the famous and the infamous buried here. The much photographed gravestone carved with the likeness of the pioneers James and Elizabeth Stephens is located in Lone Fir. The large vault and chapel was built for the Macleay family. The grave of Asa Lovejoy, who lost the coin toss to name the city, is here. The area near the Multnomah County Building is all that is left of what was once a large Chinese graveyard. At one time there were thousands of Chinese graves, but many have since been removed to China. There are over 23,000 graves at Lone Fir dating to before 1900. The earliest is 1846. Because many of the original markers were carved in wood and have disappeared with time, many graves are now unmarked. The Pioneer Cemetery office, 2115 SE Morrison, has brochures of Lone Fir that include history and maps of the cemetery. You may also obtain information on other pioneer cemeteries in the area.

Washington Park Zoo 4001 SW Canyon Rd.
Portland, Hours: 226-ROAR

The Washington Park Zoo continues to be a perennial favorite for children of all ages. In 1987 the Zoo celebrated its 100th year. The Zoo has developed a national reputation and continues to expand with new exhibits and facilities. The Asian elephant herd produces more calves than any other captive herd in the world. The Lilah Callen Holden Elephant Museum commemorates the elephant in religion, art, military history, and prehistory. There is an extensive indoor/outdoor chimpanzee habitat. The Cascade Steam and Pond Exhibit gives you a peek into a beaver hut, and you can get nose to nose with a penguin in the Penguin House. You can experience the sounds and sights of the Alaskan tundra in the Alaskan Tundra Exhibit and watch the bears frolic in their new quarters. The Zoo Train runs between the Rose Garden and the Zoo. (See RIDES)

The Zoo also offers classes and camps. Call the switchboard for more information.

VISIT A CONSTRUCTION SITE

"That's the biggest hole I've ever seen!" "How do they get that big machine down there?" "Is that a steam shovel or a steam roller?" You can usually find a construction site in downtown Portland or look in a nearby neighborhood where sewer, roads or homes are under construction. The best time to visit is weekdays, avoiding lunch hours. Bring along ear plugs and a hard-hat, and don't forget to come back again and again to watch the progress.

Puddle Walk

Put on your boots and raincoats, grab your big umbrella and head out in search of the biggest and deepest puddles. Enjoy a cup of hot chocolate and a hot bath on your return.

Glenwood Trolley Park $
Wilson River Hwy, near Glenwood, 357-3574
Hours: Open week-ends from Memorial Day through Labor Day

Only 38 miles from Portland, the Glenwood Trolley Park makes a enjoyable outing for the whole family. There is a complete 1910 style operating trolley system plus streetcars from around the world. The museum is located in a 26 acre park on Gales Creek. You can ride a trolley to a picnic area! There are even camping facilities. Make reservations for large groups.
Directions: Hwy 26 west to Tillamook Junction. Turn left on Oregon 6. Drive 12 miles on Wilson River Hwy., through Banks. Look for sign around milepost 38.

Oaks Amusement Park $
Foot of SE Spokane Street
Portland, 236- 5722
Hours: Winter, weekends, afternoon skating; daily after
Memorial Day.

Built in 1905, Oaks Park is the oldest continuously running amusement park in the nation. A long-range restoration program is in progress. It calls for returning the park to its original 1905 appearance. Restoration probably won't make too much difference to the kids, they like it just the way it is. A small train takes you through the park. There is roller skating and an antique carousel. The park has places to picnic overlooking the Willamette River.

Discovery Zone
8568 SW Apple Way
Beaverton, 297-2900
Hours: Daily, call for specific times.

They call it "Funbelievable fitness for kids!" This huge foam and vinyl indoor playground was designed by fitness experts for the 12 and under set. Kids climb foam mountains, work their way through large, open-ended tunnels, swim in giant ball baths, bounce on air beds, all at their own pace. There's even a scaled-down version for toddlers.

The philosophy here is fun free-play in a safe, challenging, non-competitive environment and to encourage children to be physically active and fit.

World Forestry Center
4033 SW Canyon Rd.
Portland, 228-1367
Hours: Daily, 10-5pm

Multi-media exhibits explain the history of forests and the forest industry in Oregon. There are interesting Tom Hardy sculptures, a talking tree, and a model sawmill. An extensive collection of wood samples from all over the world takes up almost an entire floor.

There are also changing exhibits. Many, like the wooden toy and doll house shows are of particular interest to children. Children can climb into the 1909 Shay steam engine, a logging locomotive, located outside the Forestry Center. Call for specific information about the changing exhibits and classes.

Giles Lake Area
Off Hwy 30, take 29th north to Yeon. Head northeast to Kittridege Avenue. Turn east to Front Street. Head south, making a circle out onto Nicolai Street, to Hwy 30.

This area was once a large lake and included a large pavilion, the center of activity during the Lewis & Clark Exposition in 1905. Drive by heavy metal factories, along the rail yards and close to the port action at Terminal No. 2. Quite a different environment from the early 1900's.

Incredible Universe
29400 SW Town Center Loop
Wilsonville, 682-8100
Hours: Mon-Fri 11am - 9pm, Sat. 10am - 9pm, Sun 11am - 6pm.

Billed as the world's largest electronics, appliance and computer store, you'll want to allow plenty of time for exploring this unique universe. There's everything from dishwashers to virtual reality.

At the "Kidsview Scene" children can play the latest video games and watch their favorite cartoons on a large screen for up to an hour at no charge.

Giles Lake, 1905, Oregon Historical Society Photo

RESOURCES

A visit to the Architectural Preservation Gallery, at 26 NW Second St., is a must before beginning your explorations downtown. There are exhibits, self-conducted walking tour guides, and information about Portland neighborhoods and historic buildings.

There are several good guided walking tours of downtown Portland.

Portland on Foot
John Meynink, 235-4742 $

At 93, Mr. Meynink is a living encyclopedia of Portland history. From April to September on Saturdays at 10am, Mr. Meynink begins his tours of Old Town at the Skidmore Fountain. At 2pm he conducts a Yamhill Historic District tour. He will also conduct tours on request.

Urban Tour Group, 227-5780 $

The November 1986 issue of "Oregon Geology", by Ralph Mason, explains the geology of walls and buildings in Portland.

Nature of Oregon Information Center
731-4444

Publications, maps, etc.

PARKS

The international reputation of the parks in the Portland metro-politan area is something to be proud of and, in this day of budget cuts, to protect. Those we have listed in this chapter represent only a cross-section of what is available. We simply don't have the room to include all the wonderful parks in the region. But don't stop with the parks we have featured. We suggest you get copies of the Park Bureau brochures listed at the end of this chapter and have fun exploring on your own.

NORTH

Kelley Point Park

Located at the confluence of the Columbia and Willamette rivers, this is an excellent place to watch tugs at work and the large ships leaving and coming into port. There is a large, clean beach, paved walkways, picnic tables and grills for cooking. No playground equipment.
Directions: 1-5 to Marine Drive exit. Go west past the Expo Center. Follow signs to Kelley Point Park.

Pier Park
North Seneca and St. Johns

Pier Park, which is not on the water as the name implies, con-tains the densest stand of old conifers in any Portland park. Enjoy the feel of the deep woods. On a hot summer day, the sun is bare-ly able to filter through the trees. Paved walkways throughout the park make for easy walking any time of year. The park is quiet on weekdays but tends to get busy with large picnic groups on week-ends. The park has a swimming pool, playground, sports fields, and a wading pool.

Directions: Highway 30 to St Johns Bridge. Make left on Lombard, right on St Johns Avenue, left on N. Seneca Street to the park. As you cross the St. Johns Bridge, look to the left for the tops of a large stand of fir trees - that is Pier Park.

Cathedral Park
N. Edison and Pittsburg, located under St. Johns Bridge on the east side of Willamette River.

The park is called Cathedral Park because the arches of the St. Johns Bridge overhead look like the soaring beams of a gothic cathedral. There is access to river swimming, fishing, and a public boat launch. During the summer there are jazz concerts. The park is handicapped accessible.

NORTH EAST

Peninsula Park
NE Portland Boulevard and Albina Street

Peninsula Park has a rose garden even larger than the Washington Park test gardens. There is a lovely gazebo overlooking the gardens. The playground equipment is extensive, with specific areas designed for older and younger children.

Fernhill Park
NE 37th and Ainsworth Street

A large, grassy park, Fernhill Park has wonderful hills for rolling and running and open spaces for flying kites. There is minimal, older playground equipment.

Blue Lake Park $ per car fee
20500 NE Marine Dr.
Troutdale, 665-4995

Blue Lake is 185 acres of open and developed park space. The park borders on Blue Lake, a lovely small lake that has recently reopened to the public. There is a large swimming area. You can rent paddle boats and rowboats. There are places for fishing and feeding the ducks. Play structures are located in several areas, and there is a concession stand that opens at noon. Summer concert series, call for schedule.
Note: Swim center is an additional charge, and is open when the temperature is above 72 degrees.
Directions: Located between Marine Drive and Sandy Boulevard, at 223rd, or take I-84 exit and follow Blue Lake signs north.

Rockwood Barrier-Free Park
NE 176th and Couch

This small park contains two things of special interest. There is a very large wooden play structure designed to be enjoyed by both children with and without physical disabilities. There are special swings, accessible slides, and bars and hoops low enough for a young child or a child in a wheelchair. The park also contains a PAR course, an exercise course designed to be used by both the physically impaired and the non-impaired. There is a paved trail that goes to a popular athletic field.
Note: This park is just several blocks from the 172nd Street MAX stop.

SOUTH EAST

Sellwood Riverfront Park
SE Spokane at foot of Sellwood Bridge

One of the newest additions to the Portland park system,

Greenway Park

Sellwood Riverfront park offers access to the water on the east bank of the Willamette River. There is a nice beach area and a nature walk around a small pond.

Located near Oaks Amusement Park. (See EXCURSIONS)

Laurelhurst Park
SE 39th and Stark

A large, green, hilly park with a lovely pond that is a favorite for feeding ducks year round. The playground is across the street.

Mt. Tabor Park
SE Salmon and 60th

Mt Tabor is said to be the only extinct volcano inside city limits in the United States. From the top of Mt. Tabor, you can enjoy striking panoramic views of the city. The park also has good hiking and biking trails. The city reservoirs for Bull Run water are located here. There are also picnic and playground areas.

Westmoreland Park
SE McLoughlin and Bybee

Crystal Springs Creek runs through the center of this large southeast Portland park. The stream forms two large ponds. One pond is always full of hungry ducks looking for a handout. The other, called the casting pond because it can be used for practice cast fishing, is sometimes used for small paddle-boats. The creek, as it travels between the ponds, is ideal for toy boat sailing.

Westmoreland is also a popular place for sports fans. On almost any day you can find baseball or soccer games. The lawn bowling association has built a clubhouse here and most summer weekends you can watch a game. (See SPORTS)

Directions: Go south on McLoughlin Boulevard and take Westmoreland Park exit.

Johnson Creek Park
SE 21st and Clatsop

In this serene little park, Crystal Springs Creek flows into Johnson Creek. The two streams form a peninsula. As they flow together you can see the clean water of Crystal Springs Creek flow into and disappear in the more murky waters of Johnson Creek. There are two small bridges to cross. The water flows rapidly here, so keep hold of the small adventurous types. There is also a small playground and picnic tables.

SOUTHWEST

Gabriel Park
SW 45th and Vermont

A large grassy park, Gabriel has good playground equipment, tennis courts, and a picnic area. You can usually find a softball or soccer game to watch during the summer months. There is also a small forested area with trails for hiking.

Tryon Creek State Park
11321 SW Terwilliger Blvd.
Portland, 653-3166
Open: Daily, 8-4:30

The Tryon Creek Nature House is the place to start exploring yet another well-maintained state park within Portland's city limits. The Nature House has displays, a library, and programs and classes for adults and children the year round. Within the park, there are more that 80 species of birds and small animals.

There are 8 miles of hiking trails, 3 1/2 miles of horse trails, and 3 miles of bike trails. There is handicapped access on specific trails. This is an excellent place to hike and observe nature 12 months of the year.

Willamette Park
SW Macadam and Nevada

Willamette Park borders the Willamette River and is perfect for watching boat traffic, especially small-class sailboat races in the evenings and on weekends. It is also an excellent place for kite flying because of the steady breezes coming off the river.
Note: Weekend fee per car and often very crowded on hot days.

METRO

Commonwealth/Foothills Park
SW Huntington Avenue,Beaverton

The two parks are separated by SW Huntington Avenue. Commonwealth Park has a large central pond with a paved walkway all around. Good for hot-wheels, tricycles, and beginning bike riders. The ducks and geese are aggressive. An interesting marsh is located at one end.

Foothills Park has play equipment and trails leading up to a wooded hillside.
Directions: Sunset Highway 26 to SW Cedar Hills Boulevard. Turn right on Butner Road. When you come to Huntington (between 123rd and 126th), turn left.

Jenkins Estate
Grabhorn Road, off 209th and Farmington Road.
Beaverton, 642-3855
Hours: Weekdays, 10-5

The 68-acre Jenkins Estate is a lovely place to walk, picnic, and view the Tualatin Valley. The estate consists of the original farmhouse, a stable, carriage house, pump house and greenhouse. There are flower-lined paths that meander through the woods and across a small bridge. On weekends the estate is usually used for weddings or private parties and is closed to the public. Call to get a schedule of special events, like the 4th of July celebration, that are open to the public.

Greenway Park
Beaverton

Greenway Park borders Scholls Ferry Road on the south, and Hall Boulevard on the north. The park is narrow and borders Fanno Creek which flows through housing developments. A well-paved bicycle path of over 3 miles meanders through the park. A perfect place to take a beginning cyclist, stroller, big-wheeler, even roller skates. The path also crosses several wooden bridges over Fanno Creek and passes five unusual playground structures and other sports facilities. Walking or cycling is the best way to enjoy the park.
Directions: Enter from Hall Boulevard and Greenway Street. The path is to the east of the Albertson's store. You may also enter from Scholls Ferry Road, turning north into the Parkside business complex. The path is to the east.

George Rogers Park
South end of State Street in Lake Oswego

This is a four-star park. It has everything; swimming holes with sand beaches, a small stream for wading, a small waterfall, baseball diamond, boat launch, tennis courts, and imaginative playground equipment. Good fishing spots can be found on the trails leading to Oswego Creek. The large chimney is all that is left of the first iron smelter in Oregon.

You can hike/bike from George Rogers Park to Mary Young State Park, a distance of less than 5 miles along the Willamette River. Take the path through George Rogers Park to Old River Road. There are good views of Rock Island and fishing spots, just a short climb down to the water's edge. Old River Road is flat and

Commonwealth Park

traffic is light and slow. It is an easy and enjoyable trip for young cycle enthusiasts. Paths lead into Mary Young State Park from Old River Road.

Rosylyn Lake Park
Ten Eyck Road, Sandy
Hours: 8am to 8pm

You drive through a heavily wooded area before arriving at Royslyn Lake Park. The 140 acre lake is great for swimming, fishing, and rafting. There are good picnic facilities and it is popular on weekends.
Note: Pets must be leashed.
Directions: Take a left at the light in Sandy. Follow the signs on Ten Eyck Road for about 5 miles.

Oxbow State Park
Phone: 663-4708
Hours: Daily, 6:30 am to legal sunset

Oxbow is a 1,000 acre park located 20 miles east of Portland in the Sandy River Gorge. The park has 20 miles of trails along the Sandy River and through the lush gorge. There are old-growth Douglas fir, western red cedar, as well as abundant wildlife. There are 45 family campsites. (It's a good place to try camping, because it is such a short drive from home.) There are swimming, fishing, boating, rafting, and equestrian trails.
Directions: Located approximately 6 miles east of Gresham. Follow the signs east out of Gresham on Division Street.

Mary Young State Park
Highway 43, West Linn

Mary Young State Park has hiking and biking trails. There is easy access to the Willamette River for fishing, boating and swimming .

Hagg Lake
Located seven miles SW of Forest Grove
Hours: Dawn to dusk, April to October

A favorite spot for Washington County residents, Hagg Lake offers boating, fishing, picnicking, swimming, and hiking trails. **Directions:** US 26 to Forest Grove turnoff. Then S on Oregon 47 to park turnoff.

GARDENS

Leach Botanical Garden
6704 SE 122nd Ave., (SE 122nd and Foster), 761-9503
Hours: House 10-4, Tues.-Sun.

Leach Botanical Garden is a unique botanical park built over a period of 40 years by John and Lilla Leach. It is now open for the public to enjoy. The Leachs searched the Northwest wilderness in the '20s and '30s for rare plants. The gardens, currently being restored by volunteers, reflect the Leachs' love of the Northwest and its plants.

This is a place for quiet walks. There is an old moss-covered stone cottage. Johnson Creek cuts through the property. Guided tours of the grounds are available Saturday mornings at 10am. The house is accessible and can be rented for special events. There are no playground or picnic facilities.

Note: While in the area, take a few extra moments to cross a covered bridge. To get there, follow SE Foster Road to SE 134, turn right on 134th by the fire station. The street becomes Deardorff Road. Follow the road a short distance to the Cedar Crossing Covered Bridge. There is parking on the other side if you'd like to walk it.

Crystal Springs Rhododendron Garden
On SE 28th across from Reed College, 823-3640

The 6 acres of 2,500 rhododendrons are ablaze with color from early spring through late summer. Easy walking trails wind across bridges and around the flowers and trees. A pond and stream formed by Crystal Springs Creek are full of ducks and waterfowl year round.

Note: No charge except on Mother's Day.

Japanese Garden
356 SW Kingston St.
Portland, 223-1321
Hours:Daily 10-6pm, summer; daily 10-4pm, winter

Leave the noise of the city and enter the serene world of tea gardens, moon bridges, reflecting ponds, waterfalls, and streams. The Japanese Garden, considered one of the most authentic out-side Japan, includes five traditional gardens. The Pavilion in the Flat Garden is used for special events and Japanese dancing. Call for schedule. The Tea Garden has a ceremonial Tea House built in Japan in the ancient way, with pegs instead of nails. The Sand and Stone Garden is the most abstract. It has no plants - just rocks on raked sand. Sit and listen to the sounds of waterfalls among the native mosses and ferns in the Natural Garden and walk the crooked bridge among irises in the Strolling Pond Garden.

This is not an excursion for a boisterous crowd, but a wonder-ful place for sharing quiet moments and conversations all year round.

The Garden of the Bishop's Close, Elk Rock Garden
11800 SW Military Lane
Hours: Daily, year round, 8-5pm

Bishop's Close is a 13 acre estate and garden maintained by the Episcopal Diocese. There is easy walking through beautifully manicured lawn, colorful gardens as well as areas of native vegetation. The estate includes a grove of madrona trees,a stream, ponds, and vistas over-looking the Willamette River and Elk Rock Island. Look for the "hole in the hedge" entrance to the garden from the upper parking lot. This is a place for quiet walks, talks, and thoughts.

Note: This is private property, but public access is allowed. There are no restrooms and picnicking is not allowed. Parking is limited.

Directions: Go south on Macadam, turn left on Military Road and immediately turn right on Military Lane. Garden at end of road.

Washington Park International Rose Test Garden
400 SW Kingston
Portland, 823-3636

Portland isn't called the Rose City for nothing, and here is one of the best places for views of both roses and the city skyline. The Washington Park Rose Garden, perched on a hillside in Washington Park, contains as many as 10,000 plants and 400 varieties. While the greatest variety of color usually lasts from mid to late June, the gardeners claim the more brilliant color is in the fall. The Shakespeare Garden, next to the Rose Garden, is planted with flowers and shrubs mentioned in the playwright's works.

SPECIAL FEATURES

Wading Pools

Because of budget cuts, the Portland Parks and Recreation Bureau have been unable to open all the wading pools every summer. Call the Park Bureau, 796-5193, to find out which wading pools will be open.

Swimming Pools

Abernathy	2412 SE Orange
Buckman (Indoor)	320 SE 16th

Columbia (Indoor)	7701 N Chatauqua
Couch (Indoor)	2033 NW Glisan
Creston	4454 SE Powell
Dishman	77 NE Knott
Grant	2300 NE 33rd
Montavilla	8219 NE Glisan
Mt.Scott	5530 SE 72nd
Peninsula	6400 N Albina
Pier	9341 Albina
Sellwood	SE 7th and Miller
Wilson High School	1511 SE Vermont
Woodlawn	NE 13th and Dekum

(See SPORTS for swimming holes)

Indoor Parks

A mind-saver for parents of toddlers, indoor parks are co-op organizations usually located in facilities with big spaces for climbing
and riding toys. Indoor parks offer a chance for children to get a
good workout and for parents to meet other parents. Membership
is required, and there are often waiting lists.

Fulton CC	68 SW Miles St.
Mt. Scott	5530 SE 72nd.
St. Johns	8427 N Central
First Covenant Church	4433 E Burnside
Northeast	2104 NE Hancock
Southeast	3915 SE Steele
Buckman	320 SE 16th St.
Moreland-Sellwood	1436 SE Spokane
Powell Valley	14500 SE Powell Blvd.
Bridger	7910 SE Market
Westside	16255 NW Bronson
Lake Oswego	1915 Southshore
Clackamas, Oregon city	1211 Jackson

Rose City	NE 61st and Sandy
Peninsula	6400 N Albina
Garden Home	7475 SW Olsen Rd
Inside Westside	7688 SW Capital Hwy
Hillside	653 NW Culpepper
Overlook	3839 N Melrose

RESOURCES

"Oregon State Park Guide"
Oregon State Parks
525 Trade Street SE
Salem, 97310
" Discover"
Guide to Portland Parks
Portland Bureau of Parks and Recreation
Portland Building 1120 SW 5th, Room 502
Portland,97204

Tualatin Hills Parks and Recreation
15707 SW Walker Road.
Beaverton, 645-6433

Vancouver Parks and Recreation
1009 E Mcloughlin., 206-696-8236

See DAY TRIPS for additional parks.

SPORTS

Portland is indeed a city blessed with an abundance of parks, and where there are parks, there are sports. From lawn bowling to kite flying; from lacrosse to boating; from participatory to spectator, the sporting scene in the Portland metropolitan area is limited only by the imagination and occasional rainfall. So grab your hat, horn, whistle, popcorn, pompom, and catch a game in an area park or rink. Best of all, there's no charge to watch some great competition. For more information on sports and recreational activities call:

Portland Bureau of Parks and Recreation—796-5150

Recreation For Disabled Citizens—823-4328

Tualatin Hills Parks and Recreation—645-6433

Vancouver Parks and Recreation—206-696-8236

Specific rinks or sports facilities also post activities, and don't forget your local high school athletic events.

SPECTATOR SPORTS

Lawn Bowling
Westmoreland Park
Season: Early April - Fall, as weather permits.

There is usually an enthusiastic member of the Lawn Bowling Association in the clubhouse willing to explain the game to interested observers.

Rugby
East Delta Park
Season: Spring; tournament in early May.

Lacrosse
East Delta Park
Season: Spring.

The last weekend in April, teams from throughout the Northwest compete.

Soccer
East Delta and other area parks
Season: Summer and Winter.

Leagues range in age from 6 to over 30, and in skill level from rank beginners to former professionals.

Indoor Soccer

Oregon Soccer Center $
1622 Molalla
Oregon City, 655-7529
Hours: Daily, call for specific times.

Register kids for league play. They also have a pro shop.

Portland Indoor Soccer $
418 SE Main, 231-6368
Hours: Afternoon and evenings, call for times.

Basketball
Irving Park and other area parks during summer.

Baseball/Softball
Almost any city park in the spring and summer.

Amateur Hockey

Portland Amateur Hockey runs September - April. Summer

season at Valley Ice Arena. Call ice rink for specific schedules. There is usually a charge for special events, otherwise games are free. Dress for cool temperatures.

Valley Ice Arena
9250 Beaverton Hillsdale Hwy.
Valley Plaza, 297-2521

Lloyd Center Ice Pavilion
960 Lloyd Center, 288-6073
Pee Wee Hockey

RECREATIONAL SPORTS

Skateboarding

City Skate Skateboard Park $
520 SE Salmon, 232-3988
Hours: Mon.-Thur., 11-8pm; Fri.-Sat., 10-9pm;
Sun., noon-8pm

This is an all indoor park, operated under Portland Parks and Recreation. They have thousands of feet of inter-connected ramps, including vertical half-pipe. Safety equipment is required. Call ahead for information about safety equipment, parental supervision, insurance, and other requirements. There is also a pro shop at the facility.

Ice Skating $

Call to check on open skate times

Ice Capades Chalet
Clackamas Town Center
12000 SE 82nd, 654-7733

Lloyd Center Ice Pavilion
960 Lloyd Center, 288-6073

Valley Ice Arena
9250 Beaverton Hillsdale Hwy, 297-2521

Roller Skating $

Oaks Park Roller Rink
Foot of SE Spokane, 236-5722
    This is the oldest and one of the largest roller rinks in the city and as such is a part of many Portland families' memories.

Mt. Scott Roller Rink
5530 SE 72nd, 823-3185
    A city-owned rink, this is one of the best buys in town at only 50 cents an hour, including skate rental.

For sidewalk skating, try Tom McCall Waterfront Park, Greenway Park, and city reservoirs in Washington Park and Mt. Tabor. For a listing of other roller rinks, check the Yellow Pages. Most rinks will adjust the speed of skates for young children.

Skate Rental

ICU Skate Co.
133 SW Ash, 497-9083
    This shop is located in the New Market Theater, near Saturday Market downtown. You can rent skates, rollerblades and safety equipment.

Kite Flying

The larger city parks have open areas free of kite-eating trees and wires. Particularly good ones are:
Fernhill—NE 37th & Ainsworth
Gabriel—SW 45th & Vermont

Kite Flying-Greenway Park

Tom McCall Waterfront Park—SW Front
Willamette Park—SW Macadam & Nevada
Greenway Park—Beaverton

Model Airplanes

Remote-controlled model airplane enthusiasts can now be found immediately east of and adjacent to Kelly Point Park. The wire controlled model airplanes are still located in East Delta Park.

Boating

Model Boats
    To sail homemade boats, try Westmoreland Park ponds and stream, the Lewis & Clark College Reflecting Pool, and Commonwealth Park.

Sailboats
    To watch sailboats, go to Willamette Park, the Columbia River, (off Marine Drive), and the Sailing Center, foot of SE Marion in front of Salty's Restaurant. For a good view of rowing, go to Riverplace on the Willamette.

Windsurfing: See DAY TRIPS—1-84.

Fishing

To fish in Oregon, an adult accompanying a child under 14 must have a license even if they are not fishing. Anyone older than 14 must have their own license in order to fish. Call Oregon Fish and Wildlife for more information, 229-5403. Their free publication, "Guide to Warm Water Fishing, Portland Metropolitan Area," is worth requesting. It includes a special section on teaching your child to fish.
    Many of the parks on water or with ponds allow fishing. See

PARKS and DAY TRIPS for ideas on popular fishing holes in the area.

Rainbow Trout Farm Fishing $
Off Highway 26, 7.6 miles east of Sandy, 774-0088
Hours: 7 days a week, year round.

This is a well-stocked trout farm with a lovely picnic area, and accessible paths and ramps leading to the ponds. Poles and bait are provided, and someone is on hand to help you bag and clean your catch.

Small Fry Lake
Promontory Park, 7 miles east of Estacada

This is a fishing lake for kids that is stocked by PGE. You must be 14 and under. The limit is 3 per day.

Swimming

A cool dip on a hot day? Here is a listing of our favorite swimming holes: (See PARKS for information about wading pools and municipal pools.)
• Vancouver Lake, 6 miles west, off I-5 on 4th Plain Blvd, Vancouver. See DAY TRIPS.
• Battle Ground Lake, 3 miles north of Battleground. See DAY TRIPS.
• Rooster Rock State Park, Off I-84, west of Multnomah Falls. See DAY TRIPS.
• Benson State Park, off I-84. See DAY TRIPS.
• Blue Lake Park, NE 223rd Street. See PARKS.
• Hagg Lake, off Oregon 47, 8 miles from Forest Grove. See PARKS.
• Sauvie Island, east end of island. See DAY TRIPS.

Miniature Golf

Indoor:
Chocolate Chipper
15236 SE Mcloughlin Blvd., 659-7800
   This facility has an abundance of video games, and golf.

Mr. Clean
Canby
   We found this a hard to beat combination: laundry, car
   wash, and golf!

Puttin' Around $
Vancouver Mall, (206) 253-8071. Open Mall hours.

Outdoor:
Golf-O-Rama
7127 Hwy.99
Hazel Dell, Wash.

Putt-Putt Golf Course
2400 SE 122nd
Portland, 255-5311

Sunset Golf Center
16251 SW Jenkins Rd.
Beaverton, 626-2244

BMX Tracks

Two tracks offer kids a safe place to practice their manuevers.
Such safety equipment as helmet, long sleeved shirts, and long
pants is a requirement.
Alpenrose: The track is located behind the baseball field.
Races are held from May to August, trophies and prizes are
awarded. For more information, call 640-4074.
Riverside Park, Oregon City: The track is near the Clackamas

River. To get there, take Hwy. 212 off 205, to Evelyn Street, then follow signs to park.

PROFESSIONAL SPORTS

Basketball—Portland Trail Blazers $
700 NE Multnomah, 234-9291
Season: October 30 - April. Home games are played at Memorial Coliseum.

Baseball—Portland Beavers $
1205 SW 18th, 223-2837
Season: April - August.

The Beavers are the AAA farm club of the Minnesota Twins. Come early for a game and watch batting and fielding practice. Call for more information. Various local businesses sponsor special kids' days with ticket discounts and giveaways.

Hockey—Portland Winter Hawks $
1401 N Wheeler, 238-6366
Season: October - mid-March.

While not technically a professional team, these young men, many of whom are still in high school, have been selected to train for a professional hockey career. The Winter Hawks play at Memorial Coliseum. When in town, their practices are open to the public. Call the office to get the location.

Thoroughbred Horse Racing—Portland Meadows $
1001 N Schmeer Rd, 285-9144
Season: End of October - early April.

Children are allowed to watch only daytime racing. Call the public relations office for stable tours and information about morning workouts.

Greyhound Racing—Multnomah Kennel Club $
E 223 Rd. and Glisan
Fairview, 667-7700
Season: End of April - end of August.

Children under 12 allowed only for Saturday afternoon racing. There is a paddock area where you can watch the dogs exercise.

Portland International Raceway $
West Delta Park, 285-6635
Season: Early spring - late fall.

Call for schedule of events. Some of the regular events at P.I.R. include: Bicycle racing, BMX, Drag racing, Go-Kart racing, Midget Car racing, Moto-Cross racing, 4-Wheel Mudarama, TransAm, and CART (Indy cars) races.

Portland Speedway $
9727 N Union Ave., 285-2883

Call for schedule of events. Stock cars, midget cars, and demolition derbies run on an oval track.

Woodburn Drag Strip $
7730 State Highway 214
Woodburn, 982 4461

Call for schedule of events. This is a quarter-mile track sanctioned by the National Hot Rod Association.

VIEWS

From bridges and forested hilltops to modern skyscrapers (so high you can almost touch the clouds), down to watching the traffic of two rivers and the fascinating activities of the busy port, Portland is blessed with an abundance of breathtaking viewpoints that offer a variety of scenes.

Why not take a break on a gray, cloudy day to find a hilltop to storm-watch, as the clouds roll in and out. Return to the same spot in different kinds of weather to observe all the changes. Ask your child to locate your home, or a friend's, from various hilltops in the city. Spend a quiet time making pictures out of the big puffy clouds or the spaces in-between. Remember to include a city map to point out familiar landmarks and bring your binoculars.

St. Johns Bridge
N. Philadelphia

One of Portland's most beautiful, this bridge is a national historic landmark. Park on the east side and walk across the north side of the bridge. From this gothic structure you have a helicopter high look at much of the modern Port of Portland. Watch ships load and unload their cargo. Portland is a main port of entry for Toyota Motor Co., and you can often see hundreds of cars waiting to be shipped to dealers around the northwest.
Note: An adventure walk for older children. Stay on the sidewalk and avoid rush-hour traffic. (See EXCURSIONS, St Johns and PARKS, Cathedral and Pier Park.)

Eastside Esplanade

Overlook Viewpoint
N. Skidmore Court

Turn toward the bluff, off Overlook Boulevard to Skidmore and then to N. Skidmore Court. Park and walk out across the grassy area to see the terrific view. There is a single park bench and old apple tree. Below, you can see and hear the activity of the Union Pacific Rail Yards and river traffic from the Fremont Bridge to the St. Johns Bridge. A pleasant place to picnic and enjoy the sun or, on rainy days, to watch the storms roll in over the West Hills.
Note: This view is from a very high cliff with a sharp drop-off with no fence so you need to watch little ones very carefully.

University of Portland
5000 N. Willamette Ave.

Approach via the college entrance and head toward the river. Walk toward the east, in the direction of the cliff, behind the cluster of older red brick buildings. This is the same lookout point from which the Lewis and Clark Expedition once viewed the river.

NE Marine Drive
From Gantenbein to Airport Way

Many small and large boats are moored on the Columbia River. Most of the moorages are private, but some allow you to walk down to get a closer look at the boats. At Bridgeton, turn right and head east to Marine Drive. Continue along Marine Drive where there are numerous off-road parking spaces. View the river traffic of barges, sailboats, speed boats, and wind surfers. You can also watch the landing and taking off of both commercial and private aircraft, and at times, the Air National Guard or Air Force. There are even snack vans parked along the road near Portland International Airport.

Rocky Butte
Northeast Portland

From the top, you can see all the large mountain peaks on a clear day: Mount St. Helens, Mount Hood, Mount Rainier, Mount Adams, Mount Jefferson. You'll be able to see the Columbia River, a bit of the Gorge and Larch Mountain. The Portland airport is also visible, affording a great view of planes approaching the airport. Looking west you'll spot the downtown city skyline.

Directions: Northeast 92nd Avenue to Rocky Butte Road, or on the north side of the Butte, take 91st Avenue, which winds around Judson Baptist College, with its stately white buildings and grounds. Either approach leads to the top by Rocky Butte Road.

The Grotto
Sanctuary of Our Sorrowful Mother NE 85th and Sandy Boulevard
Portland, 254-7371
Hours: Daily, except Christmas and Thanksgiving, 9:30 to 5pm

The Grotto encompasses 64 acres of woods, gardens, and shrines. You can walk or take the elevator to the upper level which offers spectacular views of the entire region.

Mt. Tabor
SE 60th between Yamhill and Division

There are several entrances to the park. Some are only open to vehicles on weekends. Take SE 60th and turn east on Salmon or Harrison. At the Salmon Street entrance is an unobstructed view of the southeast Portland area.

Further in the park, you'll wind around to the top where you have an even better view. At the top you'll find the sculpture of Harvey Scott by Gutzon Borglum, who also did Mount Rushmore.

First Interstate Bank
1300 SW Fifth Ave.

There are two public restaurants with panoramic views to the west and northeast. Not recommended for those with acrophobia!

Hilton Hotel
921 SW Sixth Ave.

Spectacular view from the 23rd floor.

SW Vista Street Bridge
Spanning SW Jefferson Street

Begin on Vista Street at SW Burnside, continue up the hill to the bridge. Park on the north side and walk across. Great view of downtown with skyscrapers at your fingertips. Note the beautiful light fixtures along the bridge.

SW Terwilliger Boulevard

For a top-ranked, top-notch view through the trees of downtown, the river, its bridges, Mount Hood, and Mount St. Helens all in one spot, go to the path along Terwilliger Boulevard just below the Veterans Administration Hospital. A citizens committee ranked this the best panorama in town. The committee ranked 127 sites, with an eye toward city preservation.

Pioneer Courthouse
Between Fifth and Sixth Avenue, Yamhill and Morrison

Except during the busiest hours, security guards will gladly take you up to the cupola on top of the building where you can rub noses with some of Portland's buildings and get a bird's eye view of Pioneer Square across the street. Also, next to each window is an old photograph or drawing depicting the way it looked if you had stood at that same window more than a hundred years ago.

Washington Park Rose Test Gardens
SW Kingston

See one of the city's most popular and photographed views. Everyone takes visitors here to show off our city. The city sponsors a free summer performing arts series here and it's a real treat to enjoy a summer concert with the backdrop of the Portland skyline looking east. As the sun sets, the buildings begin to glow.

Council Crest Park
SW Greenway Avenue

A wonderful place to watch the clouds, a good storm, or to create pictures out of clouds or the spaces in between. Good view to the east of the city skyscrapers as well as a view west of the Tualatin Valley. Fred Littman's sculpture "Joy", a Portland landmark, is located here.

SW Fairmont to SW Humphrey and back to Fairmont

You will find that these streets all connect to give a panoramic view of the city and metro area. (see METRO TRIVIA)

Washington Park, Hoyt Arboretum Loop

Pittock Mansion see MUSEUMS

Eastside Esplanade see WALKS

For other views in the region see DAY TRIPS.

ARTS

Works of art are created for many reasons and appreciated for just as many. We have focused on public art, sculptures, murals, and fountains, which surround us daily but which we may not even notice. Portland's tradition of public art dates to 1888, when the Skidmore Fountain, by Olin Wagner, was commissioned. The city wanted a place where both man and horse could drink!

As parents, guardians, and educators of children, we must help them develop a discerning eye to the art surrounding us daily in our homes, neighborhoods, and communities. This chapter was designed to be used either as a guide for a series of short tours or as a reference. Exploring public art provides an opportunity to encourage and build on prior experiences children have had with art in school and at play. Art needs our support, at home and in the community.

Tour# 1

Our first tour begins downtown at the Justice Center and takes you across Lownsdale Square to view the famous "Elk" traffic separator and to the Portland Building.

Begin at the Justice Center **(1)**, designed by the Portland firm of Zimmer, Gunsul, and Frasca and located between Second, Third, SW Main and Madison. When entering on Third Avenue, you'll find the towering free-form travertine sculptures of Walter Dusenberg. Looking up, you will discover the colorful mosaic ceiling tiles formed with pieces of fused glass, by Liz Mapelli.

Once inside, turn around to see the stained glass created by Ed Carpenter.This work is enjoyable from both the inside and outside. Located just behind the elevator is a mural of black history

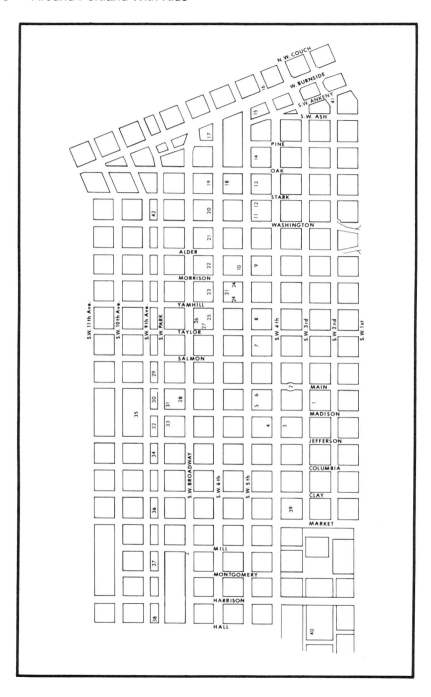

by Portland artist Isaac Shamsud-Din and a sculpture of enameled steel by Portland artist Bonnie Bronson. Walk through to the Second Avenue entrance to find the Pacific Northwest Indian Eagle, carved in cedar by a Kwakitual Indian.

Leave the Justice Center by the Third Avenue door and head down to Main Street. Crossing over to Lownsdale Square, the famous "Elk" **(2)** will be on your right. It is one of Portland's earliest fountains, done by Roland Perry in 1900 out of bronze. Notice that even animals will have a place to drink here. Head across the square to Fourth and Madison to the life-size bronze replica of the Liberty Bell **(3)**, cast by the McShane Bell Foundry. Just across the street, on the west side of Fourth, outside and just to the left of the entrance to City Hall, is the oldest work of art in Portland — a Petroglyph **(4)** of basalt, with carvings done by Oregon Country Indians. From here go to Fifth and Madison to the Portland Building **(5)**. "Portlandia", above the entrance to the Portland Building is a 36 foot sculpture, weighing 6 1/2 tons in copper on bronze, by Raymond Kaskey. The Portland Building was designed by Michael Graves, and inside is a visual arts gallery open to the public.

Tour #2

Our second tour begins at the Portland Building and takes you down the Transit Mall, across Burnside to view the Chinese Gate, then back through the US Bancorp Building onto Sixth Avenue, and up to Pioneer Square.

As you walk down the Transit Mall, pause to enjoy a refreshing drink from the famous bronze Benson drinking fountains scattered throughout the downtown area. They were designed by A.E. Doyle. Listed below are various art works to point out.

6. Interlocking Forms — sculpture, Indiana limestone, by Don Wilson. A great place to climb and take a breather. Fifth, between Madison and Main.

7. The Guest — sculpture, marble, by Count Alexander Von Svoboda. It weighs 17 tons. Fifth, between Salmon and Taylor.

8. Fountain—granite, by Carter, Hull, Nishita, McCulley, and Baxter.One of several fountains you will see by this firm. Stick your feet or hands in to test the temperature of the various pools of water. Fifth and Yamhill.

9. Cat in Repose—sculpture, Indiana limestone, by Kathleen Conchuratt. Fifth, between Alder and Morrison.

10. Thor—sculpture, copper on redwood, by Melvin Schuler. Representing the Scandinavian god of journeys and justice. Fifth and Washington.

11. Kvinneakt "Nude Woman"—sculpture, bronze, by Norman Taylor.Now famous for the "Expose Yourself to Art" poster. Fifth and Washington.

12. Forms Found in Nature and in the Tools of Men—sculpture, fountain of aluminum by Bridge, Beardles, and William Berkey. Fifth and Washington.

13. Sculpture—steel, by Bruce West. Great to knock on and hear the various tones. Fifth, between Stark and Oak.

14. Unfolding Rhythms—sculpture by Manuel Tzquierdo, 315 SW 5th

15. Fountain—steel and concrete by Carter and group(8). Take a walk behind the waterfall. Fifth and Ankeny.

16. Chinese Gate—Across Burnside. The Gate, at 39 feet tall and 50 Feet wide is one of the largest Chinese gates in the United States. Each of the guardian lions is 8 feet tall and weighs 1.2 tons. Return to Fifth and Ankeny and walk through the U.S. Bancorp Building to SW Sixth Avenue. Watch those walls of mirrors! Continue on Sixth.

17. Sculpture and Fountain—steel, by Lee Kelly.One of the best fountains for children to romp about - under, over and through the water. Sixth, between Pine and Oak.

18. Lions' Heads—a quick look through the windows of the Hong Kong and Shanghai Bank. 300 SW Sixth. Big lions leer out at you.

Transit Mall Sculpture - Interlocking Forms

19. Doors—sculpture, bronze relief, by Avard Fairbanks. Gigantic doors to the U.S.National Bank Building. The building itself is a work of art. These doors have symbolic themes - a good opportunity for a guessing game using your imagination. The doors are similar in technique to Ghiberti's "Gates of Paradise" in Florence. The doors are at the Sixth and Broadway entrance and at the Stark Street entrance. They are visible only when the bank is closed.

20. Fountain—brick and granite. Carter group(8). Wonderful for climbing on. Sixth, between Washington and Stark.

21. Sculpture — aluminum, by Ivan Morrison. Sixth between Washington and Alder.

22. Talos 2—sculpture, bronze, by James Hansen.Representing a Greek warrior. Sixth between Alder and Morrison.

23. Historic Pioneer Courthouse. At Sixth Avenue entrance there are two wooden caryatids more than 15 feet tall. The entire building is done in rich woods with high, vaulted ceilings. On the Fifth Avenue side, ask a security guard to take you up in the elevator for a view from the cupola. (see VIEWS)

24. Animal Sculptures—bronze, by Georgia Gerber. Made from 6,000 pounds of bronze, these figures line both sides of Pioneer Courthouse along Yamhill and Morrison between 5th and 6th.

25. Pioneer Courthouse Square—brick and concrete with terra cotta columns, designed by the firm of Will Martin and Associates,1984. Originally the site of Portland's first schoolhouse and later the Portland Hotel. Now a center for downtown activities and a gathering place for people young and old. Throughout the year there are special events, concerts, and plays. The Square is paved with the names of the thousands of Portlanders who supported the creation of the Square through the purchase of engraved bricks.

26. Pioneer Square Fountain—sculpture, aluminum and stone, by Robert Maki. Good place to have a leaf-floating race. When you walk by the fountain, you'll also notice that it creates an optical illusion. Pioneer Square.

27. "Ask Me"—sculpture, by J. Seward Johnson. You will frequently see people having their pictures taken with this sculpture of a man with an umbrella. Located in Pioneer Square.

Tour #3

After a brief stop at the newly constructed Portland Center for the Performing Arts, this tour will take you through the South Park Blocks and then to the Ira Keller Fountain.

28. Portland Center for the Performing Arts/ Arlene Schnizter Hall — newly constructed complex of theaters and home for the Oregon Symphony. Between Broadway and Park, Main and Madison.

29. Rebecca at the Well—sculpture - fountain, bronze and sandstone, by Olive Barrett and Carl Linde. SW Park, between Salmon and Main.

30. Abraham Lincoln—sculpture, bronze, by George Waters. Lincoln in a somber mood- the sculptor stated that this was the Lincoln of the Civil War years. Park, between Main and Madison.

31. Windows—stained glass, by David Povey, at the First Congregational Church. Povey was a glassworker who did scores of windows in both homes and churches in Portland's early days. Park and Madison.

32. Theodore Roosevelt, Rough Rider—sculpture, bronze, by Phimister Procter. It was commissioned in 1922 for $40,000. Between Jefferson and Madison.

33. Horse Cavalcade — 1982 mural, paint on cinderblock, by William Garnet. Looks like a backdrop for a Hollywood western. Park and Madison.

34. Sculpture—granite. By Steve Gillman. Forms of white granite. Good for climbing on. The sculptor brought his stone to Oregon on a large truck from California.

35. Evan H. Roberts Memorial Sculpture Mall—Displayed here are: a steel sculpture by Michihiro Kosuge; Dual Form, in bronze by Barbara Hepworth; Arlie, steel, by Lee Kelly; and two steel structures by Clement Meadmore and Richard Serra. You will also see a bronze relief of Rodin by Pierre Renoir. Courtyard of the Pacific Northwest College of Art.

36. "In the Shadow of the Elm"—environmental mosaic, granite. By Paul Sulinen. Market and Clay.

37. Farewell to Orpheus—sculpture, bronze, by Federic Littman. Park and Montgomery.

38. Fountain—Tom Hardy. Portland State University campus.

Head back downtown and turn east on Market Street. Walk down to Fourth Avenue to the Ira Keller Memorial Fountain **(39)** (Forecourt). Take a rest and cool your feet in the many streams of water. More than 13,000 gallons of water a minute cascade over the high concrete walls. Designed by Angela Danadjieva for Lawrence Halprin. Third and Clay.

Note: The water in the fountains in Portland is not recycled and while wading in fountains is not actively encouraged it is not discouraged.

Downtown, there are three more exciting fountains to explore. The Lovejoy fountain **(40)**, another fountain by Halprin and Associates, in the Portland Center off SW First and Hall, behind the Portland Center Plaza. The Skidmore Fountain **(41)** by Olin Warner at First and Ankeny was mentioned earlier.

O'Bryant Square **(42)** not only has a wonderful fountain to sit beside but many fine concerts are performed here during the summer months. Designed by Danile, Mann, Johnson, and Mandenhall, it is at SW Park and Washington.

Now off to discover some decorative murals in the downtown area

• Bighorn Sheep—paint on concrete by Greg Brown. They even have shadows. SW Tenth, at Salmon.

• The Audience—paint on wood, by James Gardiner. 1530 SW Yamhill.

• The Rose—paint on concrete, by Jonathan Gibson. SW Thirteenth, at Washington.

BY CAR
There is still a great deal of art to be seen, but it is best reached by car.

Architectural Treasures

Northwest
• Figures and Phrases—chalk on concrete, by Tom Stefopoulos. The drawings were done in 1948 and have been preserved in relatively good condition. Located under the Lovejoy ramp to the Broadway Bridge at NW Twelfth. Surrounded by lots of old cobblestone streets.
• Butterfly—paint on brick, by Joe Erceg. NW First at Davis.
• Pittock Mansion—3229 NW Pittock Dr. (See MUSEUMS)
• Temple Beth Israel—1931 NW Flanders.

Southwest
Washington Park is not only a beautiful park to be enjoyed by all, but it also contains numerous pieces of artwork to notice the next time you visit.
• The Frank Beach Memorial Fountain—at the Rose Test Garden, steel, by Lee Kelly and David Cotter. Beach nicknamed our city the "Rose City". The fountain is a delight to dance around, and in, for people of all ages.
There are numerous beautiful sculptures located in the Zoo. They are hands-on, climb-on sculptures for kids and adults.
• Bear and Nursing Cubs—marble,by Beniamino Bufano.
• Lion—bronze, by Phimister Procter.
• Sleeping Badger—serpentine, by Tom Hardy.
• Totem Pole—by Chief Dan Lelooska.
Follow the Park Street entrance in Washington Park to see the famous bronze sculpture of Sacajawea by Alice Cooper.
• Multnomah Mural—by Daniel Florea. Believed to be the largest mural in Oregon at 400 ft. long and 25 ft. high. It spans three buildings. SW 35th and Multnomah Blvd.

Transit Mall Fountain

• New Market Theater—50 SW 2nd Ave. Built along the lines of an Italian palazzo. This was the site of the first concert by what is now known as The Oregon Symphony.
• Multnomah County Library—801 SW 10th Ave. Inside is one of the grand stairways in town.
• Jacob Kamm Mansion—1425 SW 20th. Built in 1971 *1871* as the city's first great mansion. It is the only surviving example of French Second Empire style. Its owner was a partner in the Oregon Steamship Navigation Co., at one time the largest business in the West.

Northeast
• Sculpture—"Capitalism" by Larry Kirkland. A 17-foot-high classical Greek Ionic column made of 50 marble coins emblazoned with famous people's quotes about money. You'll find this splendid piece of art work at the main entrance of Lloyd Center Mall.

Southeast
• Sculpture—steel by Lee Kelly, Bonnie Bronson, and assisted by Duniway School students. 7700 SW Reed College Place.
• Benjamin Franklin—sculpture, sandstone. A statue of that famous man. 5405 SE Woodward, Franklin High School.
• Harvey Scott—sculpture, bronze. Located at the top of Mt. Tabor, 60th, between Division and Yamhill. By Gutzon Borglum, who also sculpted the famous presidential faces at Mount Rushmore.
• The Crystal Pallets: Defense of Light—sculpture, glass by Richard Posner. The panes of etched glass with photos tell of remarkable events in our nation's political life. A must for political history students. Located at the Multnomah County Elections Building, SE Eleventh and Morrison.
• Buckman Neighborhood Mural —acrylic on cinderblock, by Geoffrey Clark and Buckman School students. Another display of childrens' art. SE Twelfth and Morrison.
• Fountain—steel and brick by Bruce West. St. Francis Park, 1136 SE Oak.

SCHOOLS, CENTERS, THEATERS

Portland is blessed with many fine and talented artists. We've included a sampling of schools and centers which offer classes for children in fine arts, crafts, dance, music, and theater. Call for a schedule of classes.

Pacific Northwest College of Art $
1219 SW Park, 226 4391

Classes in fine arts and crafts.

Northwest Film Study Center $
1219 SW Park, 221 1156

Classes in filmmaking, video, and photography.

Portland Civic Theater School $
1530 SW Yamhill, 248-9158

Classes in theater and production.

Lake Oswego Community Theater $
368 S. State, Lake Oswego, 635-3901

Classes in drama.

CITY ARTS PROGRAM THROUGH THE PORTLAND BUREAU OF PARKS AND RECREATION

Community Music Center $
3350 SE Francis Street, 823-3177
Classes and private lessons in voice, instrumental music, and appreciation. Preschool and up.

Metro Performing Arts
6433 NE Tillamook, 823-3660

Call for info on classes.

Multnomah Art Center $
7688 SW Capital Hwy., 823-2887

Classes in dance, movement and art.

Children's Museum $
3037 SW Second, 823-2227

Classes in music, art and crafts.

Performances and artworks can be seen locally in numerous galleries and performing centers. Following is a list of theaters that frequently have productions of special interest to children. There are too many galleries in Portland to list here. Watch the newspaper and media for exhibits and performances that might be of special interest to your child. Call theaters and galleries to get on their mailing lists. Don't forget to check with your neighborhood high school and local college or university for concerts, art shows, and theater productions.

Tears of Joy Puppet Theater $
400 W Evergreen Blvd.
Vancouver, 206-695-3050

Recognized as one of the nation's most outstanding puppet theaters, the Tears of Joy Puppet Theater tours throughout the US. Call for schedule of performances and puppet workshops.

Ladybug Theater $
Oaks Park, SE Spokane at foot of Sellwood Bridge, 232-2346

Improvisation and audience participation make these productions of children's classics a favorite for all ages.

New Rose Theater $
904 SW Main Street, 222-2487

Offers several youth performances a year.

Carousel Company Theater for Children $
710 NE Holladay, 238-0012

A professional group that offers original theater throughout the year.

Portland Youth Philharmonic $
Portland, 223-5939

Symphony and brass ensembles.

MUSEUMS

Oregon Museum of Science and Industry, (OMSI) $
1945 SE Water Ave.
Portland, 797-4000
Hours: Mon.-Wed., 9:30-5:30pm; Thur.-Fri., 9:30-9pm; Sat.-Sun., 9:30-5:30pm; extended summer schedule.

OMSI continues to get better and better. It is definitely one of the best places in Portland for entertainment. The new OMSI has six exhibit halls where you can reach out and touch a tornado or experience life on a space station, build a bridge or match wits with a computer. Each hall has a different theme, and each adjoins a specialized laboratory and activity where you can play scientists and test the theories demonstrated in exhibits. Traveling, hands-on exhibits stay three to four months, and are always worth an extra visit or two.

The "Old OMSI," across from Washington Park Zoo, is now the education resource center, where OMSI's education programs continue to expand.

Murdock Sky Theater
OMNIMAX Theater
1945 SE Water Ave.
Portland, 797-4600, 1-800-957-6654
Hours: Varies, call for show times. Sky theater shows begin on the half hour; OMNIMAX, shows begin on the hour.

Astronomy and laser light shows in the Sky Theater.

The OMNIMAX Theater is the first in Oregon. With a five-story domed movie screen, and a 30-degree tilt to the seating area, it literally surrounds you with sight, sound and motion.

Oregon Art Institute (Portland Art Museum) $
1219 SW Park
Portland, 226-2811
Hours: Tues.-Sat., 11-5 pm; Sun. 1-5pm; 1st Thurs., 11-9pm,
4-9pm free.

Exhibits of special interest to children are the fine Northwest Coast Indian Art and the Asian galleries. Watch for touring exhibits. (See ARTS)

Portland Police Historical Museum $
1111 SW 2nd, Justice Bldg.
Portland, 796-3019
Hours: Mon.-Thurs., 10-3 pm.

Uniforms, photographs, and memorabilia tell the fascinating history of police work in Portland.

Children's Museum $
3037 SW 2nd
Portland, 823-2227
Hours: Mon.-Sun., 9-5pm.

A museum with exhibits especially for children to touch, manipulate, and experience. There are changing exhibits as well as popular, permanent exhibits like the time tunnel, grocery store, customs house, and infant room. Dozens of art, music, and move-ment classes are held in the museum annex. You can even schedule a special birthday party at the museum. Call for informa-tion. (See RESOURCES)
Note: The Museum has definitely outgrown its facility. Efforts are underway to find a new location. Keep informed on how you can help support them.

Oregon Historical Society $
1200 SW Park
Portland, 222-1741
Hours: Tues.-Sat., 10-5pm, Sun., 12-5pm, Closed: Mondays.

The Oregon Historical Society's focus is on regional history. Downstairs are rotating exhibits, while on the second floor are dioramas on Indians of the Oregon country and life-like displays of life on the Oregon Trail. The bookstore, near the entrance, has one of the most complete collections in the state about the Northwest, including children's books.
Note: Handicap access at the Broadway entrance.

Stevens-Crawford House
Clackamas County Historical Museum $
603 6th Street Oregon City, 655-2866
Hours: Wed.- Sun., 10-4pm.

The Historical Museum is in a 1908 house and is noted for its fine collection of Native American artifacts. There is also an entire room of antique dolls.

Clackamas County History Museum $
211 Tumwater Dr.
Oregon City, 655-5574
Hours: Mon.-Fri., 10-4pm; Sat.-Sun., 1-5pm.

Exhibits pertaining to county history. Allow at least 45 minutes to go through the museum.

End of The Oregon Trail Preview Center
Oregon Trail Foundation, Oregon City, 557-1151

This building complex, in the shape of three 50-foot tall covered wagons, is located geographically at the end of the Oregon

Trail. The exhibit offers a gallery and theatre honoring the Oregon Trail Pioneers.

McLoughlin House $
73 Center Street Oregon City, 656-5146
Hours: Tues.-Sat., 10-4:pm; Sunday, 1-4:30 pm.

The McLoughlin House was the retirement residence of Dr. John McLoughlin, an officer in the Hudson's Bay Company (see Fort Vancouver), founder of Oregon City and "Father of the Oregon Territory". The house was built in 1846, and was moved from Third and Main in 1909. Many of the furnishings and artifacts are from the McLoughlin family or date from his residence in the house. For groups and guided tours, call ahead.
(See WALKS, Oregon City Promenade)

End of the Oregon Trail Interpretive Center $
5th and Washington St.
Oregon City, 657-9336
Hours: Daily, 10-4pm, Sun. 12-4pm.

This museum graphically describes the arduous trip on the Oregon Trail and the arrival of the pioneers in Oregon City. Slide shows, artifacts, and excerpts from pioneer journals bring light to this dramatic period of history.

Cowboy Museum
729 NE Oregon St., 731-3333
Hours: Wed.-Fri., 11-5pm; Sat.-Sun., noon-5pm.

Chuck wagon, tack room and cowboy-theme exhibits operated by the Cattlemen's Heritage Foundation.

Pittock Mansion $
3229 NW Pittock Drive Portland, 248-4469
Hours: Daily, 12-5 pm.

French renaissance-style mansion built during 1909-1914 by Henry Pittock, founder of the Oregonian newspaper. The house is a showpiece of fine local craftsmanship. Several of the original craftsmen actually assisted in directing the restoration of the house in 1964, when the City of Portland purchased the estate to prevent it from being torn down. Tours are guided. The grounds are open daily and provide a spectacular view of the city and mountains. The Wildwood Trail crosses the property. (See WALKS) The Gate House has recently been renovated and turned into a tea room serving light lunches. (See EXCURSIONS) During the Christmas season, the entire house is decorated.
Directions: Head west on Burnside. Signs indicate the turn for the Pittock Mansion.
Note: Watch for special seasonal events.

Washington County Historical Society Museum
17677 NW Springville Rd., 645-5353
Hours: Mon.-Sat., 10-4:30 pm

Exhibits trace the history of Washington County from early Tualatin Valley Indians (Atfalati), missionaries, and pioneer farmers, to the present-day high tech companies. The exhibits are self-guided, but there are tours for groups. The museum also has a library for community and historical research.
Directions: Follow Hwy. 26 to 185th, turn right; follow signs to Washington County Museum. Located on the campus of Portland Community College, Rock Creek Campus.

Kidd's Toy Museum
Parts Distributing Inc.
1300 SE Grand Ave., 233-7807
Hours: By appointment.

Bi-planes, horse-drawn hook-and-ladder wagons, logs trucks, mechanical banks, and fleets of automobiles and ships are only a small sample of the toys represented in this amazing collection numbering in the thousands. The cast-iron toys date between the 1870's and the 1940's. Most are American made.

Oregon Maritime Center and Museum $
113 SW Front Ave.
Portland,224-7724
Hours: Summer, 11-4pm., Tues-Sat; winter, 11-4pm Fri-Sat.
Open Sunday 11-5pm.

Opened recently, this small museum is an effort to remind Portlanders of their maritime history. Guides will answer questions and explain the various displays. Call in advance to arrange tours for groups.

Architectural Preservation Gallery of Portland
26 NW Second Ave., 243-1923

A good first stop for those interested in learning something about Portland's architectural history. There are changing exhibits about Portland's historic homes and buildings, self-guided walking tours, neighborhood information, and a helpful staff.

The American Advertising Museum $
9 NW Second Ave.
Portland, AAM-OOOO (226-0000)
Hours: 11-5pm, Wed- Fri., 12-4pm., Sat.-Sun.

The American Advertising Museum is one of the newest museum additions to the Portland area and is the largest museum devoted to advertising in the nation. Exhibits include a historical time line of advertising from the 1600s through the era of television. You can follow the development of an ad campaign and see some of the many advertising artifacts like the classic Burma Shave signs. Radio and TV commercials play continuously in a special section of the museum. The museum offers a wonderful opportunity to show children the role of advertising in our culture.

Aurora Colony Ox Barn Museum and Aurora National Historic District $
Aurora, 678-5754
Hours: Wed-Sat, 10-4:30pm. Sun., 1-4:30pm.

Oregon's history of communal societies goes back to 1856 when the Aurora Colony was founded by the German/American followers of Wilhelm Keil. The Ox Barn Museum contains artifacts and information about this fascinating pioneer communal culture. The town of Aurora is a National Historic District. There are many antique shops and restaurants in the old buildings. See CALENDAR for special events at the Museum.

Haggart Observatory $
Clackamas Community College
19600 S. Mollalla
Oregon City, 657-6958, ext. 352
Hours: 8pm-midnight on cloudless Wednesdays, Fridays and Saturdays.

Bybee-Howell House and Agricultural Museum (See DAY TRIPS, Sauvie Island)

Fort Vancouver and Officer's Row (See DAY TRIPS, Vancouver)

Gilbert House Children's Museum (See DAY TRIPS, Salem)

See DAY TRIPS for other museums in the region.

TOURS

Children love to know how things are made or where they come from. The questioning begins early and hopefully never ends. The tours included here are but a sampling of what is available in the metro area. There are many places that are not geared for "tours", but will accommodate a request from a small group or for a family visit. On your own, try your local bakery or an interesting looking business or factory.

Most facilities included in these tours have special requirements. It is a must that you call well in advance of your planned visit. Some restrict tours to certain ages and group size. Most tours are conducted weekdays during regular business hours. Some tours have individual guides who will direct your group. Always consider your group's age, number, and interest when selecting and planning a tour.

FOOD TOURS

Skychef
7210 NE Alderwood
Portland, 251-3360
Hours: Weekdays, 1-4 pm.

See the entire process of preparing meals; from the sink to the ovens to the trucks. These meals are used on airplanes and in some local hospitals.

Hoody
5555 SW 107th
Beaverton, 646-0555

Watch the processing of peanuts into peanut butter and

syrups, as well as the packaging of dry and roasted peanuts and sunflower seeds.
Note: Age: First grade and up. Group size: Max. 15. Time: One hour. Tours conducted February through May.

Steinfeld's Products
10001 N Rivergate Blvd.
Portland, 286-8241

See the fine art of pickle making; from vine to fermenting tanks and into jars. This facility also makes relishes and sauer-kraut.
Note: Age: Sixth grade and up. Group size: small.

Nabisco
100 NE Columbia Blvd.
Portland, 240-7600

Here you can observe the production of crackers and cookies, from the raw materials to the finished product.
Note: You must call the first week in October to schedule tours for that school year. Tour days are Tuesday and Thursday, October-May. Age: Sixth grade and older. Group size: 25 maximum. Under two hours.

Alpenrose Dairy
6149 SW Shattuck Road
Portland, 244-1133

See the complete process of milk production from cow to car-ton. On unscheduled visits you can look through the windows and watch the 4pm milking. The grounds of the dairy are lovely and there are frequent events scheduled here. (see CALENDAR) Little League ballgames are played here throughout the summer, and during Christmas, many of the small buildings in the little village are open to the public. The old Opera House shows movies, and there is a Storybook Lane and Santa's House.

Note: Call the first week in September to set up guided tours for the school year. Age: Grades 1 and 2. Under two hours. There are adult-only tours available the first Tuesday of the month. Reservations are required.

Franz Bakery
340 NE Eleventh
Portland, 232-2191

See flour mixing, baking, cutting, and packaging. A great place to enjoy baking smells—you even get to sample! You don't need an appointment to stand at the window on 12th St. and watch the bread come out of the ovens. Bread is baked 24 hours a day, Monday-Saturday, so just drive by and see if something is cooking. Don't visit on an empty stomach!

Note: Call before February to schedule tours. Length: under two hours. Age: Second grade and up. Group size: Max.20.

Oregon Candy Farm
48620 SE Hwy 26, Sandy, 668-5066
Hours:Weekdays, 9-5pm;Sat.-Sun., 12-5pm. Reservations are not required for small group.

Watch candy-making.

McDonalds, Wendy's and Burger King Restaurants

Call your local McDonalds, Burger King,or Wendy's for a "behind the scenes" tour of the fast food industry.

Frito Lay
4808 NW Fruit Valley Road
Vancouver, (Portland No.) 283-5113

This tour shows you how potato chips are made, from the potato to the package. Call to get specifics on group size and ages.

MEDIA TOURS

Several local stations have guided tours for school age children. We have included live audience programs under EXCURSIONS.

KATU Channel 2
2153 NE Sandy Blvd.
Portland, 231-4222

The tour is combined with a visit to a local show broadcast.
Note: Call at least one month in advance. Age: six and older. Tour lasts 20 - 30 minutes.

KGW Channel 8 and Radio
1501 SW Jefferson
Portland, 226-5000

Call a month in advance. Age: Fourth grade and up. Tour length is one hour.

KEX Radio
4949 SW Macadam
Portland, 225-1190

Call a week in advance.

Oregonian
1320 SW Broadway
Portland, 221-8337

Tour the news room and various departments of Portland's

only daily newspaper. You can visit the editorial desks and the press plant where the paper is printed. You may get a copy hot off the press.

Note: Call at least six weeks in advance. Age:12 and up. Group size: 10-15. Length: over two hours.

INDUSTRY TOURS

United States National Bank of Oregon
321 SW Sixth Ave.
Portland, 275-7938

Tour the bank departments, the vault, and see the Rose Festival Crown. The tour also includes some information on the architectural history of the building.

Note: Call a week ahead. Tours conducted before 9:30 am.

Esco Corporation
2141 NW 25th Ave.
Portland, 228-2141

In this steel mill, observe the melting, pouring, and casting of metals. Hardhats and safety glasses are issued and wearing old clothes is a must. Outside, note the world's largest cast steel sculpture, "The Flogger", a tribute to the steel industry, by Frederic Littman.

Pendleton Woolen Mills
Washougal, Wash., 226-4801

See the manufacture of Pendelton material.

Note: Age 12 years and older for school groups. No age restrictions on family tours. Tours weekdays, 9,10,11, and 1:30. Some limitation on group size.

Directions: I-5 North to Vancouver or I-205. Take Hwy. 14 east to

Washougal. You will see the signs for the Pendleton Woolen Mill at 15th St. Turn left off highway.

Pendleton Woolen Mills
Milwaukie, 654-0444

See the manufacture of shirts and robes.

Note: Tours given 10am and 1pm. No age restrictions on family tours. Group tours, call in advance.

Port of Portland

Reservations for tours of the marine facilities and the airport must be made well in advance. The Port of Portland also has a traveling van program that visits classrooms with a slide show presentation and program about port activities.

Marine Facilities/Industrial Lands Tours
231-5000 ext. 208

This tour will show you Portland's waterfront at work. You visit the Portland ship repair yard, see the largest grain elevator on tidewater west of the Mississippi, and visit the container loading facility at Terminal 6. You also tour the industrial area. On this tour you stay on the bus.

Note: This tour is for school groups or organizations. Children must be third grade or older. Group size: minimum 15. You must provide your own bus.

Saturday Summer Tours
231-5000 ext 208

This tour takes you through the terminals, ship repair yards, and the airport aboard a specially chartered bus. The tour takes about 2 1/2 hours.

Portland International Airport Tours
231-5000 ext. 208

This tour includes walking through the entire airport with a guide. You will see all the airport operations except boarding a plane and visiting the tower. There is also a slide show.
Note: Tours: Mon.-Sun. Age: Third grade and above. Tour lasts about 1 hour.

HOSPITALS

Most hospitals in the metro area offer tours to groups, and to children scheduled to enter for hospitalization in the near future. The tours generally include walks through various departments such as medical labs, pediatrics, emergency rooms, nurses' stations, as well as a view of a hospital room. Don't limit yourself to just the ones we have included. When calling to arrange a tour, ask for volunteer services.

Emanuel Hospital
2801 N Gantenbein
Portland, 280-3200

Tour is geared to the age of the group. You will also visit the Lifeflight helicopter pad.

Portland Adventist Hospital
10123 SE Market
Portland, 251-6114

Classroom discussions stressing health education geared to specific age and understanding.

St. Vincent's Hospital
9205 SW Barnes Rd.
Portland, 297-4411

Special packet given at the end of the tour with health and safety items including " Mr. Yuk" stickers.

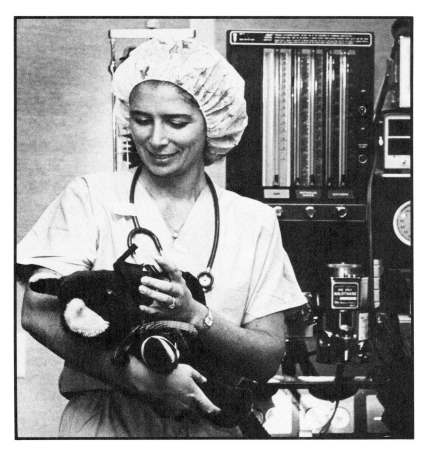

Emanuel Hospital

Providence Medical Center
4805 NE Glisan
Portland, 230-1111

Tours geared to age and interests of group. Grades 2 and up.

MISCELLANEOUS

Mounted Police Horse Stables
1036 NW 9th
Portland, 823-2100

Place for children to meet and learn about the care and training of the police horses. Call ahead to arrange for tour.

Oregon Humane Society
1067 NE Columbia Blvd.
Portland, 285-0641
Hours:Daily 9am-5pm, closed 12-1pm.

The Oregon Humane Society features kennels, a modern cattery, a lively barnyard, a wildlife refuge and pond, and one of the oldest pet cemeteries in the nation. Tours are designed to be appropriate for children ages 4 and older. Included is a program on responsible pet ownership and kids are given time to interact with animals.
Note: Tours Mon-Fri., 10 - 4pm. You must reserve at least two weeks in advance. Tour last about 1 hour.

Van Calvin Manikin Restoration
16950 NW St. Helens Rd.
Portland, 621-3007
Hours: Call ahead to arrange tours.

See the step by step construction and restoration of store

manikins. To get there take US 30, West; 12 miles from downtown Portland.

Portland Opera Costume Shop
1302 NW Glisan
Portland, 224-6687

The shop has more than 8,000 costumes from various Portland Opera productions. You can see the creation of a costume—from sketches to the finished product. We suggest that you visit five or six weeks prior to the opening of an opera, then return to see how it all comes together. The shop staff will also visit schools to put on a demonstration, bringing their wigs, make-up and costumes.

National Weather Service
5420 NE Marine Dr. Portland, 281-1911

There are rooms full of gauges, recorders, maps, and screens that monitor the state's weather. You'll see machines that measure the height of clouds and one that counts the length of time that the sun shines. This is the first place to receive information of pending natural disasters. Television and radio stations call here for hourly weather information. The facility welcomes informal visits of younger children, during regular business hours, if they are well supervised.
Note: Age: Sixth grade and up. Group size: small.

US Post Office
715 NW Hoyt
Portland,294-2257

On a guided tour, you'll see all the automatic equipment that moves the mail from your mailbox to its destination.
Note: No tours in December. Age: 8 and up. Group size: five or more. Tour lasts about 90 minutes. Informational brochures on post office available before tour.

See also EXCURSIONS and DAY TRIPS

Carousel Courtyard

RIDES

Portland offers many ways for one to travel about. Whether you want to go by land, sea, or air, up or down, or around and around, Portland has the ride designed for just what you had in mind.

CAROUSELS

Jantzen Beach Center, 289-5555 $
Hours: Open daily, year round. Mon.-Fri. 12-9pm, Sat. 10-6pm.,Sun.11-5pm.

This is the largest Parker carousel in the West, with 72 horses, and was built in about 1904. Located in the Mall area.

World Forestry Center $
Washington Park, 228-1367
Hours: Open daily from 10 to 5pm during the summer vacation months. After school begins, the carousel is open only on weekends, while weather permits.

This 1914 outdoor carousel, with wooden lions and 54 horses, originally toured a fair circuit in the East.

Oaks Amusement Park $
Foot of SE Spokane, 236-5722
Hours: Open summers from noon to dusk. Winter- weekends only.

A 1920 Spillman, with two chariots and 64 animals in pairs.

Burlingame Burger King $
7601 SE Barbur Blvd.,245-1238

Built in 1900, this carousel has two-seated horses and ostriches.

ELEVATORS

To elevate your spirits on those down days, try an elevator ride. You'll find the fastest, the most nauseating, the longest, and the best outdoor and indoor elevators listed here. Just about any to fit your fancy!

Oregon City Municipal Elevator
Seventh Avenue and Main Street, Oregon City
Hours:7am to 7pm: Closed Sundays

Cross under railroad tracks through a cool tiled tunnel to the elevator. The elevator operator also acts as a guide. At the top observation point, you get a panoramic view of the Willamette River, south to the falls and north to the I-205 Freeway.

200 Market Street ("The Black Box")

The elevator goes from the first to the 19th floor at very fast and smooth pace. Rated the smoothest, but rather boring compared to some others.

1515 SW Fifth Avenue

Located within an atrium, this ride takes you up nine floors in a very elegant fashion. The atrium is a pleasant place to spend a quiet moment on a rainy day. Rated the best indoor glass elevator.

First Interstate Bank
1300 SW Fifth

Rated the fastest! A restaurant and deli on the 28th floor have a panoramic view of the city.

PacWest Center
1211SW 5th

This ride is an ear-popper.

US Bancorp
Fifth and Burnside

There are three sets of elevators: floors 1-17, 18-30; and the expresses -from 1-30 and 30-43. It travels a swooshing 30 feet-per second. This elevator ride is rated the longest.

Portland City Parking Garage
Between Fourth and Fifth, Alder and Washington

This is one to press your nose against to get the full effect. For just 60 cents you can spend an hour going up and down on one of the city's best outside glass elevator rides. If you enter on the blue track you can ride from the 10th floor down. If you enter on the orange track you'll get nine floors of pure thrill.

Pioneer Court House
Fifth, between Yamhill and Morrison

This antique elevator has to be one of the fanciest around.

Red Lion/Lloyd Center
1000 NE Multnomah

Spectacular view of mountains and the city from this 15-story outside glass elevator Located near Lloyd Center MAX stop.

Neurological Sciences Center, Good Samaritan Hospital
1040 NW 22nd

This elevator talks, but it has a little trouble saying "floor four. "

Embassy Suites Hotel
900 SW Washington Sq. Rd.
North Side of Washington Sq.

This is an inside, glass-enclosed elevator that gives a quiet, smooth ride up from the lobby.

BUS

Tri Met Services $

For some interesting bus rides which will give you wonderful views of the city and Metro neighborhoods, try these:

No. 31 Estacada, 231-3231

One of Tri-Met's longest, this route is over 33 miles. It goes from the Portland Transit Mall through Clackamas Town Center to Estacada the long way.

No. 12 Sherwood-Barbur-Sandy, 231-3112/3212

This is another long ride, over 30 miles. This trip takes you through Washington County, to downtown Portland, and out to northeast and Airport Way. You'll see many different views of Portland,airport traffic, and the metro area.

No. 5 Interstate-Hawthorne, 231-3205

This ride will take you from Vancouver, Washington to the Transit Mall, and out to southeast Portland. You will cross two rivers and travel in two states!

No. 24 Halsey, 231-3124

Travel from Troutdale into northeast Portland to the Gateway Transit Center. From here, board MAX for a ride into downtown Portland.

No. 63 Washington Park Zoo, 231-3263

Painted by Scott McIntire, you can't mistake this bus. It leaves from Fifth and SW Washington downtown and goes to the zoo.

For more information on bus trips contact:
Call-a-Bus System—231-3199
Call for Current Fares—233-3511
Handicap Information—231-4952
Most trips turn around at the end of the line and return by the same route. Try creating your own special return trip.

HELICOPTER/AIRPLANE

Hillsboro Helicopter $
1040 NE 25th, 648-2831

It's the home of "Skyview Traffic Watch". On Saturday you can get a 5 minute helicopter ride for $12.50.

Airplane $

Airplane rides are quite expensive and most of the local small airports do have charter services. For an older child, a flight in a small plane over Mt. St. Helens is a thrill difficult to top! Mt. St.Helens flights are available at most of the area small plane airports.

BOATS

Ferry Crossings
See DAY TRIPS, Canby, I-5 South and Coast Trip #1, Westport.

Columbia Gorge Sternwheeler $
PO Box 307
Cascade Locks, 374-8427 or 374-8619
Portland, 223-3928
Season: Portland-October thru mid-June. Cascade Locks-mid-June thru September

Ride on a replica of a turn-of-the-century sternwheeler. The trip usually takes about two hours. In Cascade Locks, the Sternwheeler travels up and down the Columbia River in the Gorge. In Portland, the Sternwheeler offers spectacular views of the city from the Willamette River.
Directions: Take exit No.44 off I-84 east to reach Cascade Locks. Sternwheeler is moored in Marine Park. (see DAY TRIPS, I-84)
Note: Amtrak stops at Cascade Locks if you want to leave the car at home and combine a boat and train ride. Call Amtrak or the Columbia Gorge Sternwheeler ticket office for current schedules.

TRAINS

MAX $
22-TRAIN (228-7246)

MAX is the latest addition to Portland's transportation scene. This electrically operated light-rail system runs from the downtown area across the Steel Bridge, through NE Portland and out to Gresham.

Traveling by light-rail is a quiet, relaxing way to see the downtown area and east county. The spacious cars travel an average speed of 20 mph in the city and up to 55 mph along the Banfield

Freeway into east county. Riders can board and exit the light-rail train at any of the 27 stations along the 15 mile route. Riders can transfer between MAX and bus lines.

You might combine a MAX trip with a visit to Lloyd Center (see SPORTS), Rockwood Barrier Free Park (see PARKS),or a stop at the new Farmer's Market in Gresham. The trip to Gresham is approximately 45 minutes.

Amtrak $
Portland, 273-4866

For a short, delightful train ride, board either at the Union Station in Portland, and ride across the Columbia River to the train depot in Vancouver, the Burlington Northern Station at the end of West 11th Avenue. Or reverse the trip. The ride is less than 30 minutes, but you will get the feel of travel by rail.

Northwest Live Steamers
Shady Dell Park, Molalla
Hours: Opens 1st Sunday in May and operates every nice Sunday until October. Noon to 5pm.

These are small trains pulled by real steam engines. You can ride on the small cars around a park-like setting. Bring a lunch and have a picnic. Two times a year, usually in July, this is the home of the Steam Up Celebration which brings train buffs from all over.

Directions: South on I-5 from Portland, take the Woodburn exit,and head for Molalla. Go through Molalla. Just past the city limits, the road comes to a T. Turn right. Next you will encounter two y's; stay to your left each time. The second Y has a sign advertising Northwest Live Steamers. The park is approximately 2.2 miles from the center of Molalla.

Washington Park Zoo Train $

The Zoo Train operates at the Washington Park Zoo during normal Zoo hours. During the winter months, the trains operate only on weekends, weather permitting. You can board at the Zoo and get off at the Rose Test Gardens if you wish, reboard later, and return to the Zoo. Or you can begin your trip at the Rose Gardens.

On your Zoo Train trip you will see behind-the-scene activities of the Zoo and lots of forest and park surroundings.

Lewis & Clark Railway Co. $
Battle Ground, Wash.
Call for schedules, 206-687-2626

Riding in restored, historic train cars, at a leisurely pace of 15 mph, excitement mounts as riders pass through a 340-foot long tunnel and cross the Lewis River on a 50 foot high trestle. This section of track was laid in 1903.

On arriving at Moulton Falls Park, there is the option of catching a later train back to the depot, or limiting the stopover to a quick 20 minutes while the engine is switched. The park is picnic perfect.

Directions: From I-5 or I-205 take Battle Ground exit and follow signs to downtown Battle Ground (approximately 10 miles.) Depot is on Main Street at railroad crossing.

Phoenix and Holly Railroad
Small steam powered trains (see DAY TRIPS, Canby)

Glenwood Trolley Park (see EXCURSIONS)

TAXI

Bring a bit of New York to Portland. Take a short trip through downtown or your neighborhood. Have your children ever had the opportunity to ride a taxi in Portland? When did you take your last taxi ride?

Broadway Cab—227-1234 $

New Rose City Cab—282-7707 $

Portland Taxi—256-5400 $

Radio Cab—227-1212 $

TROLLEYS

Vintage Trolley

The cream and red trolleys are replicas of the "old 503" used on the Council Crest line between 1904 and 1950. They have wood interiors and cane seats, but modern safety equipment. The trolleys travel along the MAX line downtown, across the river to Lloyd Center and back. Service is on weekends and everyday from the day after Thanksgiving through Dec. 24.

Willamette Shore Trolley
222-2226
Hours: Weekdays, beginning mid-March; From June 1, Thurs.-Sun., 10-4pm.

No replica, but the real thing, is the bright yellow 1913 trolley that runs between downtown and Lake Oswego. The route follows the Willamette River past parks and stately residences, across two trestles and through a tunnel.

Portland passengers board at SW Moody Avenue and Sheridan Street, near the Marquam Bridge. Lake Oswego passengers board at the corner of State Street and Terwilliger Blvd. It is important to call ahead for group reservations.

RECREATION

Malibu Grand Prix $
9405 SW Cascade Blvd.
Beaverton, 641-8122
Hours: Mon.- Sat., 11-5pm

When the light turns green, "put the pedal to the metal" and you're off! Around and around the track you'll speed, until you cross the finish line with the checkered flag flying. A perfect, safe place to carry out that Mario Andretti race car fantasy, whether you are young or old. The Indy 500 cars come in adult as well as kid sizes.
Note: Child must be 4' 6" tall to drive cars.

SHOPS

Let's face it, we are a culture dependent on large shopping centers and huge chain stores. Our kids think that all food comes pleasantly wrapped in colorful packages, and they seldom experience anything but the impersonal efficiency of these cavernous rotundas of consumerism. We have included a sampling of some of Portland's most interesting smaller stores to encourage you to rediscover, with your children, the fun and surprises that these places have to offer. After visiting some of the larger stores we suggest you begin to explore on your own the many small shops that abound in Portland.

Remember, these small stores are all in business, so try to go at off hours, when shopping is not so hectic, and in very small groups. It would seem a good idea, also, to notify the proprietor if you intend to visit with a group.

Buy something if you can, particularly if you spend a great deal of time in the store. For grocery stores it might be fun to plan a meal ahead of time. Or just pick out interesting looking foods to take home to sample.

When visiting ethnic grocery stores, prepare the children ahead of time for cultural differences in choices of foods. This is a good opportunity to teach that which is strange to one culture may be a delicacy somewhere else. Many of the small grocery stores are family operated and frequently serve as community centers for a particular ethnic group. Often the clerks speak little or no English and you'll have to get by on lots of smiles. This can be a fun or frightening experience for a child, depending on how you handle it.

SPECIALTY STORES

Nature's
3449 NE 24th, 288-3414
4000 SW 117th, Beaverton, 646-3824
5909 SW Corbett, 244-3934
6344 SW Capitol Hwy., 244-3110
3016 SE Division, 233-7374

A health food store gone gourmet! Nature's is the largest store in the Portland area devoted to natural products and remedies. Here you will find incredibly artistic arrangements of chemical-free fruits and vegetables. There are fresh and dried pastas of every shape, size and kind. You can grind your own peanut butter. Food items are in bulk and more traditional packaging. Nature's also carries some non-food items such as kitchen wares, books, and toiletries. The Division Street store has a kids play area and a full-service restaurant. It is a place that proves that shopping can be fun!

Anzen Importers
736 NE Union, 233-5111

Japanese foods and imported goods; watch the butcher prepare fresh sashimi.

Fong Chong
301 NW Fourth Ave., 223-1777

This is a good place to explore Chinese food products. The store has a large selection of foods from all over the Orient. There is also dim sum carry-out and a dim sum restaurant next door.

Becerra's Elda Spanish Foods
3022 NE Glisan, 234-7785

This Spanish market carries food, and a selection of Spanish magazines, greeting cards, records, video and audio tapes, pinatas and candies.

Le Panier
71 SW Second St., 241-3524
Yamhill Market, 110 SW Yamhill, 241-5613

This is a French bakery with flair, and the SW Second location is the largest store. Here you will find a tremendous assortment of breads in amazing shapes and sizes. Delicious pastries are baked all day long in the huge ovens out front so kids can watch the loaves of bread going in and coming out of the ovens; the smells are wonderful, and it is impossible to leave without something.

Boyd's Pet Shop
5540 E. Burnside, 232-6830

Boyd's is one of the oldest and most pleasant pet stores in town. They carry all kinds of small animals: kittens, fish, birds, mice, and rabbits.

Pet N' Pond
14405 SW Pacific Hwy. Tigard, Canterbury Square, 620-1226

Well known for its great selection of exotic birds, fish and reptiles; includes many items for small pets.

Holland Feed, Pet, and Garden Supply
12250 SW Broadway Beaverton, 644-3400

You will find yourself in the midst of bales of hay, sacks of grain, and other animal feed at the Holland Feed store. This store serves as a food and equipment supplier for farm animals, large and small. You can learn what to feed a baby pig or buy a harness for your pet pony. There is also a small pet store and garden shop.

Hollywood Costumes
3121 NE Sandy, 235-9215

Enter and take a giant step into the world of make-believe. This is a great place for children to explore the looks of past and future. You can create the most awesome costumes; be anything or anyone you want to be. The store has racks of costumes and accessories, masks, and makeup.

Oregon Craft & Floral
4401 NE 122nd, 257-0704
Oregon City Shopping Center at I-205 and McLoughlin, 655-3488
8620 SW Hall Blvd., Beaverton, 646-8385
2101 E Burnside, Gresham, 646-1469

The name says it all, This is the A to Z of craft and floral supplies.

R.B. Howell
630 N.W. 10th, 227-3125

You can find almost anything you are looking for in this 100,000 sq.ft. craft supply store: feathers, ribbons, dried flowers, and miniatures for doll houses - the list goes on and on.

Callin Novelties-Magicians' Supplies
412 SW Fourth St., 223-4821

In addition to supplying everything an aspiring magician could desire, Callin Novelties sells games, novelties, and party items. Best of all, between 11-5:30, Monday through Friday, and 10-4:30 on Saturday, there is a magician in the store to demonstrate tricks

and help you pick out items.
Note: A small, Adults Only section.

Apple Music
225 SW First Ave., 226-0036

Whether you are putting together a rock band or discovering the joys of sound, a visit to Apple Music is a must. Guitars in every shape, size, and color line the walls. Gigantic sound systems are stacked to the ceiling. Drums, cymbals, and keyboards are at your fingertips. This is a store that allows reasonable "hands on" experience, and you don't need to worry about noise.

99¢ or Less
11945 SW Pacific Hwy., #240, Tigard, 684-7830
18105 SW Tualatin Valley Hwy., Aloha, 591-1222

This store has a large section of odds and ends, trinkets and trifles, baubles and beads, all at just the right price, and for the entire family.

Bridgetown Hobbies and Games
3350 NE Sandy, 234-1881

Almost every game of strategy imaginable, as well as books on games, can be found at the Military Corner. The store also sells models, metal figures, and the paints and supplies to go with them. There are computer games, games of fantasy, and science fiction.

Portland Sports Card Company
2401 NE Broadway, 284-7126

Haul out your old baseball card collection, or if you don't have one, here is the place to start. There are expensive collector's cards (the ones your mother threw away when you were 12), cur-

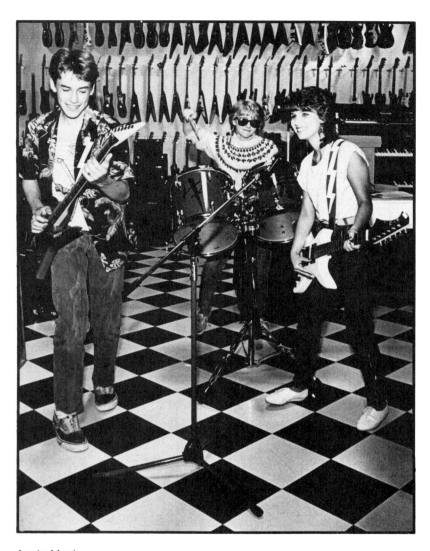

Apple Music

rent cards, card albums, and sports magazines. This is also a place to buy, trade, and sell.

Hippo Hardware and Trading Company
1040 E Burnside, 231-1444

A second-hand store with "hands-on" philosophy. There are four floors of old and new tools and antiques of many varieties. School tours available.

Quintana's
139 NW Second Ave., 223-1729
818 SW First Ave., 228-6855

The stores reflects the diversity in western American Indian art. While it looks almost like a museum, it is a gallery and what you see is for sale. Take young children firmly in hand. Tours are offered, provided arrangements are made well in advance.

Stark's Vacuum Cleaner Sales and Service
107 NE Grand, 232-4101

In the corner of the store, at the entrance you will find a vacuum cleaner museum! Yes, a collection of over 100 pieces of equipment, some dating to the early 1900's, designed to make easier the age-old task of cleaning the floor.

Portland Bagel Bakery and Delicatessen
222 SW 4th, 242-2435

From behind a glass partition you can watch the entire production of bagels.

Cal's Pharmacy
2520 East Burnside, 233-5217

This drugstore has a skateboard department managed by teen-agers. After school and on weekends, you can get your questions answered by the real experts. There is also a newly installed soda fountain.

RESTAURANTS

We have included only a few eating adventures, selected for their uniqueness and special attraction to children.

Carnival Restaurant
2805 SW Sam Jackson Parkway, 227-4244

This restaurant is an old Portland family tradition. It has carousel animals to sit on, and animal high chairs for the tots.

Old Wives' Tales
1300 E. Burnside, 238-0470

This is a smokeless restaurant with a children's playroom.

Old Spaghetti Factory
715 SW Bancroft, 222-5375

Overlooking the Willamette River, this is a comfortable place to dine with children.

Organ Grinder Pizza
5015 SE 82nd, 771-1178

You won't have to worry about your children making too much noise here. They will have big competition at the Organ Grinder. The Organ Grinder Pizza has the largest pipe organ of its kind in the world and it plays while you eat.

AFTERNOON TEA

The English custom of afternoon tea is just beginning to become popular in Portland. Usually served between 2pm and 4pm, it consists of finger sandwiches, pastries, muffins, perhaps fruit and, of course, tea. This is an outing for older children and party manners.

Heathman Hotel
SW Broadway and Salmon, 241-4100
Hours: 2-4 pm daily

Tea is served in the hotel's richly decorated lobby. Reservations suggested.

The Governor Hotel
SW 10th and Alder, 224-3400

Tea is served from 2:30-4:30p.m., Mon-Fri.

Pittock Mansion Gate Lodge Tea Room
3229 NW Pittock Drive, 823-3627
Hours: 11:30-3:30, weekdays.

With advance notice, the staff will make a special preparation for children. They will serve groups with reservations.

Pomeroy House
20902 NE Lucia Falls Road
Yacolt, Wash., 206-686-3537

Special occasion teas. (See DAY TRIPS.)

ICE CREAM

Rose's Ice Cream
4444 NE Fremont, 282-4615

A 1950's era ice cream parlor with original flavors of home-made ice cream.

Fairley's Pharmacy
7206 NE Sandy Blvd., 284-1159

This is an old fashioned 11 stool soda fountain.

Paulsen's Pharmacy
4246 NE Sandy, 287-1163

This soda fountain opened in 1918.

Farrell's Ice Cream Parlor Restaurant
1613 NE Weidler, 281-1271

A wild and crazy kind of place. You can order a sundae that will feed a whole crowd and have your birthday announced with shouts and drums.

SHOPPING CENTERS

As parents of young children know, a shopping center is one place to go in bad weather. This is particularly true when you go at off hours to avoid crowds and kids have a bit more freedom to exorcise those rainy day demons.

All shopping centers are good places for window shopping and people watching. Most have some type of fountain or interesting sculptures. We list a few of the local shopping centers that offer special features of interest to kids.

Jantzen Beach Center
I-5, Jantzen Beach Exit

Antique Carousel, pet store (See WALKS for additional ideas).

Clackamas Town Center
1200 SE 82nd St.

Ice Capades Chalet — ice skating (see SPORTS); restaurants overlooking ice rink; pet store.
Note: The elevators are hard to find and it is difficult to get from one level to another with strollers and wheelchairs.

Lloyd Center
Between NE Weidler and Multnomah

Lloyd Center Ice Pavilion — ice skating. (See SPORTS)

Pioneer Place
700 SW 5th

Three floors of bright, shinny shops under a glass roof. There are national specialty outlets, including The Nature Company. A sky bridge connects Pioneer Place to Saks Fifth Avenue. In the lower level you'll find a food hall selling a wide selection of international dishes.

Galleria
921 SW Morrison

Sky bridges to parking lot; high, brightly lit open space in center of building; long escalator ride between floors.

New Market Theatre/Skidmore Fountain Building
50 SW Second

New Market Theater is a beautifully restored building that was originally designed as a market with a theater on the upper floor. (See EXCURSIONS) There are restaurants and small shops here now. The newly opened Skidmore Fountain Building across the street also has small shops.

CHILDREN'S BOOK STORES

For a city of its size, Portland has an unusually large number of children's bookstores and general bookstores with children's sections. We have included only bookstores that primarily carry books for and about children. All have staff that know what children like and are very helpful.

Children's Place
1631 NE Broadway, 284-8294

This store carries books and one of the most complete collections of tapes and records around.

Book Barn For Children
4507 SW Watson, Beaverton., 641-2276

Here you will find a broad selection of books for children.

School Daze
11945 SW Pacific Hwy., Tigard, 624-9085

Good selection of educational books, games and toys for children and teachers.

Children's Books
79 NW Miller, Gresham, 661-5887

Carries a large selection of hard cover, paperbacks and also delightful cards and gifts.

Ginger & Pickles Bookstore for Children
425 SW Second St., Lake Oswego, 636-5438

Maintains a large selection of foreign titles, as well as popular current titles and classics. The shop also has a laminating machine.

Powell's Books For Kids
Cascade Plaza, Hwy. 217, Progress Exit
Beaverton, 671-0671

In addition to Powell's City of Books at 10th and W. Burnside, which has a large children's new and used book section, this outlet is devoted entirely to children's books. They also have audio and video tapes, and literary stuffed animals.

CHILDRENS TOY STORES

The stores listed below carry a large selection of educational, high quality, and imported toys. If you are looking for something creative or just a little different try one of these stores.

A Child's Play
907 NW 23rd, 224-5586

Country Tales, Ltd.
229 E. Main, Hillsboro, 693-9838

Finnegan's Toys and Gifts
922 SW Yamhill,221-0306

DAY TRIPS

An adventure chosen from this section of Around Portland with Kids will consume the larger part of a day. We have selected locations that generally will take no more than 2 hours of driving one way. Most are much less. We have grouped the trips in geographic areas. In some cases we have simply identified a destination. In other instances we have selected a major highway or route, and indicated the points of interest along the way. We do not intend that you do all the activities in one trip, but make numerous day trips to the area. We suggest you use a map to calculate the driving time before taking off. Our suggestions are designed to be a starting point, if you are in an area that has a visitors center, stop in and find out other places of interest in the area.

The success of a day trip will depend on many factors, including how well your children ride in a car. In addition to physical comfort, you will need to think of entertainment for longer trips. Have each child maintain a backpack with some special travel items. Books, tapes,and car games go a long way toward keeping the peace.

You might add state maps and an extra set of keys to the travel pack discussed at the beginning of this book. And, of course, every car should have a well stocked first aid kit. Take the extra minute to think about your plans and include those special items like a kite, binoculars, or beach toys. It may make your trip just that much more enjoyable!

VANCOUVER

Vancouver, USA, is a city with a rich history. Founded as a fur trading post in 1824, it is the oldest continuous settlement in the

Pacific Northwest. A day of exploration should include some of the places listed below. For a more extensive guide of the Vancouver area, pick up the map and guide titled, "Vancouver USA" at the Visitors Bureau, 303 East Evergreen Blvd., Vancouver.

Fort Vancouver, Officer's Row
1501 E Evergreen Blvd.
Vancouver, 206-696-7655
Hours: Daily, 9 to dusk.
Admission fee charged at Fort entrance.

Take a trip back in time at the Fort Vancouver National Park. As you enter the area you'll see, on your left, Officers' Row. The houses were constructed between 1849 and 1906 and served as homes for officers stationed at the military post. The houses were recently acquired by the city of Vancouver and will be restored to their original external appearance.

Below Officers' Row is Vancouver Central Park, a wonderful large, open, grassy park with an old fashioned bandshell. The park has a play structure, picnic area, and many summer activities. There is a bicycle trail that winds through the area.

The Fort Visitors Center, located in the park, has a slide show to give you historic background before going into the fort. There is a small museum and a gift shop.

The fort is a reconstruction of the 1825 Hudson's Bay Trading Post. Guided tours are given year-round, and, during the summer, guides are often dressed in period costumes. Frequently, you will see demonstrations of settlement crafts by blacksmiths, bakers, and weavers. There are special events throughout the year. Call for a schedule.

Directions: I-5 to Mill Plain exit. Turn right on Mill Plain and follow signs to Fort Vancouver.

Clark County Historical Museum
1511 Main Street
Vancouver, 206-695-4681
Hours: Sun.- Tues., 1-5pm.

Board the Pullman car and pretend you're traveling crosscountry. The ticket is free at this museum operated by the Fort Vancouver Historical Society. An entire room is devoted to railroad memorabilia. Other exhibits include a turn-of-the-century doctor's office, a country store, and print shop. Group tours available for a small fee.

Esther Short Park
8th Street and Esther
Vancouver

The oldest public square in Washington state, this 5-acre site has a number of unique features. A towering slide has left parents weak-kneed for generations. A railroad engine is planted in the middle of the park. Sculptures, victorian rose gardens, and the Slocum House, constructed in 1867, give a sense of the city's early culture.

Old West in Miniature
Corner of 15th and Harney Streets.

Located in the backyard of one of the most colorful houses in the metro area, this miniature of Dodge City is fun to visit if you are in the area.

Old Apple Tree Park

Said by some to be the oldest apple tree in the Northwest, there is a romantic tale about its origins. When a young sailor left his sweetheart in England, she gave him apple seeds from the dessert served at his farewell party. The young woman asked the sailor to plant the seeds when he reached the Northwest Territory. Legend has it that in 1826 he did just that.

Once surrounded by freeway, the tree now has a small park of its own. To reach it, take I-5 to Highway 14, walk through a refurbished railroad underpass along Columbia Way. There is parking across the street at Waterfront Park. Look for an Apple Squeezing Festival in October.(See CALENDAR)

Tears of Joy Puppet Theater See ARTS, and CALENDAR for Vancouver events.

VANCOUVER / BATTLE GROUND AREA

Vancouver Lake Park
Six miles west of I-5 via Fourth Plain Blvd.
Vancouver

This is the largest lake in the metropolitan area and is the site for a wide variety of water sports: sailing, swimming, skiing, canoeing, windsurfing and rafting. Rental boats are available. The area is well landscaped, with large grassy areas for sunbathing and picnicking. There are nature trails for short hikes, and the park has a clear view of Mt. Hood.

Battle Ground State Park

This park has a spring-fed lake for swimming and fishing. There are horse and hiking trails, camping, and a big children's playground. It is a popular destination on a hot summer day.
Directions: Follow signs out of Battle Ground.

Lewis & Clark Railway (See RIDES)

Pomeroy Farm
20902 Lucia Fall Rd.
Yacolt, 206-686-3537

Hours: Pomeroy House • Mon.-Sat., 10-5pm., Sun., 1-5pm. Pomeroy Farm • Open the first full weekend of each month from May to October.

The Pomeroy House has a well-stocked gift shop of English imports and offers craft classes and special holiday teas. Children particularly like the Teddy Bear Picnic given in August and the hay rides in September and October. Reservations are required. Write or call to get on their mailing list for special events.

The Pomeroy Farm recreates 1920s farm life. The farm is open to the public with a "living history" tour of a working blacksmith shop, farm craftsmen, antique farm machines and tools, and gardens.

Directions: 60 minutes from Portland, and about 15 minutes from Battle Ground. Call for directions.

I-5 NORTH

Ridgefield Wildlife Refuge

Trails wind through swamps and forests in the Ridgefield Wildlife Refuge. There is good birdwatching, so bring binoculars.

Directions: I-5 to the town of Ridgefield. Follow signs to Wildlife Refuge.

Hulda Klager Lilac Gardens $
Woodland, 206-225-8996

Hulda Klager was a well known plant hybridizer who began to work with lilacs about 1905. By 1910 she had developed 14 new varieties of lilacs, and was rapidly becoming recognized nationally for her work. Her home and gardens have been designated a National Historic Site.

The beautiful gardens are open all year-round and there is usually something in bloom. One of the best times to visit the gardens is during Lilac Week, the last week in April and the first week in May. The house and out buildings have been restored and made into a museum. They are usually open only during Lilac Week and by appointment. There are picnic tables and public restrooms.

Directions: I-5 North. Take the Woodland exit no. 21. Drive through Woodland. There are signs for the gardens.

Lewis River Recreation Area

There are eight major parks on the north shore of Merwin, Yale, and Swift reservoirs east of Woodland. These parks have swimming, boating, picnicking, and some have camping facilities. For more information and camping reservations call Pacific Power and Light recreation department,243-4778.

Directions: I-5 North. Take the Woodland exit no.21. Follow the Lewis River Road, State Highway 503.

Chief Lelooska
5618 Lewis River Road
Ariel, Wash., 206-225-9522

In a Kwakuitl Long House, Chief Dan Lelooska and his family fascinate audiences with traditional Northwest Coast Indian dances, songs and stories. Call for current schedules and reservations. The Totem pole at the Washington Park Zoo was created by Chief Dan Lelooska.

Ape Caves

This is an adventure for kids and strong-hearted adults. Ape Caves is one of the longest intact lava tubes in the continental US. It is believed that the 12,810 foot long tube was formed by an eruption of Mount St. Helens in 86 AD. It was named Ape Caves after a local outdoor group called the "St. Helens' Apes" who originally explored the tube. They named themselves after the mysterious "Sasquatch".

Note: The temperature in the tube is usually around 42 degrees so heavy clothes are needed. You also must carry at least two dependable sources of light!

Directions: I-5 North, exit 21. Take State Highway 503, Lewis River Road. Outside of Cougar take Road 83, then turn on to 8303. Ape Caves is located 10 miles from Cougar.

Mount St. Helens National Volcanic Monument
3029 Spirit Lake Hwy
Castle Rock, 206-274-4038
Open Daily 9 5pm.

The new monument presents an audio-visual cultural and geologic history of the mountain. There is a walk through a model of a volcano. The telephone number is a recorded announcement which includes a daily mountain visibility report.

Directions: I-5 North, Exit 49, Castle Rock. Follow signs approximately 5 miles from I-5.

Wolf Haven $
3111 Offut Lake Road
Tenino, 206-264-4695
Hours: June-Sept.,Daily, 10-5pm.
          Howl Ins, June-Sept., Fri. 7pm.
          Oct.-May, Fri.-Sun., 10-4pm.

Wolf Haven is a sanctuary for homeless and unwanted wolves from all over the United States. The foundation provides educational programs and conducts research aimed at the preservation of wild wolves. This is an opportunity to see and learn about this fascinating animal.

Howl-ins are held on Friday nights in the summer. There is story telling, music, a marshmallow roast, and an opportunity to howl with the wolves!

Directions: I-5 to Tenino.

I-5 SOUTH

Champoeg State Park
Champoeg exit off I-5

Located on the east bank of the Willamette River, this was the site of the first organized government in the Pacific Northwest in 1843.

A visitors center features displays of the early life of the Calapooya Indians, fur trappers and settlers. Adjacent to the visitors center is the Manson Barn built in 1862. The home of the Newells, original Champoeg residents, is nearby. This was built in 1852. Also located in the park is the Pioneer Mother's Memorial Cabin, built in 1929 and based on descriptions of original pioneer cabins.

Along with the historical sites, the park offers numerous recreational activities including picnic sites, ballfields and hiking and biking trails through the park and along the river bank. During the summer, don't miss the Champoeg Historical Pageant. (see CALENDAR)

Western Antique Powerland Museum
3995 Brooklake Road NE
Brooks, 393-2424

This open-air museum was organized by a group dedicated to the preservation of antique farm machinery and related farming methods. Most of the equipment sits outside for close up viewing. With close supervision you can even climb on some of the pieces. Each summer there is the "Great Oregon Steam-up". During this time, all of the machines are fired-up and you can see flour milling, log sawing, tractor pulls, and blacksmiths. (see CALENDAR)
Directions: Exit 263 off I-5

Schreiners' Iris Garden
3625 Quinaby Rd.
Brooks, 393-3232

The nation's largest iris grower. Flowers bloom mid-May to mid-June. Tours only during blooming season.

Bike/Ferry Trip
Willamette Mission State Park, Wheatland Ferry, and Williamson State Park

Fifteen miles north of Salem a pair of state parks on opposite sides of the Willamette River offer excellent family hiking and biking opportunities. There is a bike trip between the two parks and across a ferry. Either backtrack or use a car shuttle system.

Begin at Willamette Mission State Park. To reach the park from Salem, head north on Hwy 219 (River Road N.) to Wheatland Rd. (about 4 miles), then follow signs for 8 miles, through hop and mint fields, to Willamette Mission Park. The park offers six miles of hiking trails that wind through the park and along the Willamette River. There are two warm-water lakes where you can fish.

Take the Wheatland Ferry to visit the second park. There is a well-signed bike path north to the ferry landing. The ferry makes its 5 minute trip from 6am -9:45pm. Bikes and pedestrians ride free. From the other side of the river continue on Wheatland Road two miles west (slightly uphill) to Maud Williamson State Park. Here you'll find plenty of shade among the towering Douglas fir.

Enchanted Forest $
7 miles south of Salem, exit 248 off I-5, Phone: 363-3060
Hours: March 15 • Sept.30, 9:30-6pm, daily

This storybook wonderland is a delight for both young and old. Set in a deep forest one follows a trail through the land of beloved storybook characters from Humpty Dumpty to Alice in Wonderland. There's even a rabbit hole large enough for an adult to slip through. The Haunted House has real cobwebs and there is a thrilling ride around Ice Mountain. During the summer months the Fair Weather Theater performs children's plays daily. There are a number of restaurants within the area as well as picnic tables.

Silver Falls State Park
26 miles East of Salem, 873-8681

A treasure among Oregon state parks, this 8,600 acre area offers many delights. Stop at the visitors' center to pick up maps of the area. There are 14 waterfalls in Silver Creek Canyon. A six-mile loop trail (partially paved) leads you past 10 waterfalls. The South Falls is a highlight as it cascades over 177 feet. Further east on State 214, one can view the North Falls which flows over a volcanic outcropping. You can also walk behind the falls for a unique vantage point. Certain areas of the park are open year round and visitors can enjoy hiking, biking, camping and the horse trails.
Directions: Take I-5 South to Hwy 22 East. Turn on to Hwy 214.

Agriculture Tour
Harrisburg

The Willamette Valley is one of the Northwest's richest agricultural areas. Acres of wheat, corn, hops, and mint alternate with fruit and nut orchards,and fields of grass and sugar beet seed crops. Take this tour during different seasons to get the total picture: Watch the planting in the spring and the harvesting in the fall. Stop off in the city park in Peoria for a picnic and to dangle your toes in the cool Willamette River.
Directions: To make the loop, exit off I-5, west to Hwy 34. Take

Peoria Road south to Harrisburg. Out of Harrisburg, head back north on 99E or 99W to connect to Hwy 34. Go west to I-5 to complete the loop.

Covered Bridge Tour
Linn County, Albany, Oregon

Oregon's covered bridges are picturesque, adding country charm to the area. As in the past, they serve as a protective device from the notorious rainy weather, their design increasing the lifespan of the bridges by protecting the wooden trusses. In Linn County, there are eight bridges within a short distance of each other. To begin your tour, stop at the Visitors Center, 435 W. First Ave. in Albany to pick up the brochures "Covered Bridge Country" and "Oregon's Covered Bridges." Use these brochures for specific directions to the bridges.

Just 20 miles east of Albany off Hwy 226, you'll travel over paved "back country" roads to these bridges. There are five located along Thomas Creek on Kelly Road, Goar Road, Jordon Road, Richardson Gap Road and Camp Morrison Drive. Three more bridges cross Crabtree Creek on Hungry Hill Drive, Richardson Gap Road and Fish Hatchery Road. One of the most picturesque covered bridge settings and our favorite is at Larwood Wayside off Fish Hatchery Road. Here Larwood Bridge crosses Crabtree Creek and Roaring River. There is an old waterwheel nearby which adds to the charm. This is a perfect place to skip a rock or two or dangle your feet at the rivers edge.

A few miles up Fish Hatchery Road is Roaring River Park. A great place for a picnic, the park has hiking trails and covered picnic facilities. Continue a few more miles on Fish Hatchery Road to Roaring River Fish Hatchery. Open year round, you can feed hungry fish, from the tiny fingerlings to full grown salmon.

Linn County Museum and Moyer House $
Park Street, Brownsville, 466-3390
Hours: Wed.- Sun., 11-4pm.

This museum contains artifacts of life in Linn County from pioneer days to the present. There are many fine old buildings in town, so save time for a stroll.

National Wildlife Refuges

There are three National Wildlife Refuges located in the Willamette Valley. These refuges were established in the 1960's as wintering areas for dusky Canadian Geese. A visit to any one of these refuges provides a closer look at many different wildlife species in their protected habitat. Binoculars or a spotting scope is a must. Include a good birdbook to help with identification. Have children make drawings or take notes on their observations. Make return visits during different seasons to observe the changes in wildlife and habitat. Visitors are encouraged to contact headquarters to get up-to-date information on current wildlife viewing opportunities.

William Finley Refuge is located 12 miles south of Corvallis, off Hwy 99W. This is the largest refuge with 5,325 acres. Here you'll find almost all species of birds common to the Willamette Valley.

Ankeny Refuge is located 12 miles south of Salem, off I-5, and has wildlife characteristic of the Willamette Valley bottomland and agricultural areas.

Basket Slough Refuge is 12 miles west of Salem, off Hwy 22, and has a habitat typical of the valley's irrigated hillsides. Morgan Lake and Basket Slough provide habitat for many aquatic species.

SALEM

Salem, Oregon's state capital is located 40 miles south of Portland, near the 45th Parallel, halfway between the North Pole and the Equator. Watch for signs marking the exact spot as you approach Salem on I-5.

Here are some places to visit in Salem.

Capitol Building and Grounds
Court Street., 378-4423

The buildings and grounds are open to the public year round. You may wander around by yourself or take a guided tour which includes viewing the legislature when in session. Beside the hustle and bustle of politics, there is also plenty of art to enjoy.

In the rotunda there is a large bronze replica of the Oregon State Seal. Colorful murals and sculptures depicting events in Oregon history decorate the building and grounds. The crowning effect is the "Oregon Pioneer" atop the capitol building. Cast in bronze, by Ulric Ellerhusen, this heroic figure represents the spirit of Oregon's early settlers. It is finished in gold leaf, stands 24 feet and weighs over 8 tons. From the fourth floor of the capitol building you can take 121 steps up to stand under the "Oregon Pioneer."

Mission Mill Village
1313 Mill St.
Salem, 585-7012

Mission Mill Village is located a few blocks from the capitol on four and a half acres in the heart of downtown Salem. Back in 1896, Thomas L. Kay built a mill where the first worsted cloth woven west of the Mississippi was produced. Guided and self-tours of the historic mill and other surrounding historic buildings and homes are available.

Bush House and Park
600 Mission St. SE
Salem, 363-4714

Build by Asahel Bush in 1877-78, the founder of the Oregon Statesman Newspaper, this home contains the belongings of the Bush family. Many of the items in the home are one of a kind, shipped around Cape Horn from the East Coast and Europe. The barn, rebuilt in 1963, serves as a community art center. The once open green pastures surrounding the Victorian estate are now a municipal park that is a great place for a picnic or quiet stroll. A Soap Box Derby track is also located within the park.

Mill Creek Stroll

From Bush Park head north up Church or High Street to bridges over Mill Creek. Here there is easy access to trails that run along the stream for several blocks in either direction. Here each year you can see the phenomenal sight of the returning steelhead and salmon as they swim up stream to spawn. (see CALENDAR)

Gilbert House Children's Museum $
116 Marion St. NE
Salem, 371-3631

Many interesting exhibits and activity areas, including The Water Room, Inventor's Workshop, Outer Space Theater, a Walk in the Woods, Children Around the World. Special activities are offered each month. For groups of 10 or more, you must reserve ahead to get special rates. Closed Monday.
Directions: Take Salem Parkway exit from I-5; the museum is on the riverfront; park just north of the Marion Street bridge.

CANBY

The small community of Canby, about half an hour drive south from Portland, makes an outing with enough variety to please both the young and old in your family.
Directions: Take 1-5 to the Canby exit. Follow signs to Canby. This is a circle route. If you prefer to take the ferry first, take the Stafford Road exit off the freeway. Head south to Mountain Road. There will be signs for the ferry.

Canby Depot Museum
Canby, 260-2980
Hours: Sat., Sun. 1-4pm.

The Canby Depot, built in 1873, is Oregon's oldest railroad station.

Swan Island Dahlia Farm
Canby, 266-7711

You have to see it to believe the color in these fields of dahlias. The Dahlia Festival is the first and second weekend in September.
Directions: Left off Holly Road. Look for signs.

Three Rivers Farm
2525 N. Baker Drive
Canby, 266-2432

Three Rivers Farm is a totally organic farm that has produce and u-pick strawberries. Families are welcome.
Directions: Continue past the Dahlia Farm, turning right, continue to the end of the road.

Phoenix and Holly Railroad $ donation
2512 N. Holly
Canby, 266-3581

The Phoenix and Holly Railroad is a small-gauge steampowered railroad that winds through fields of u-pick flowers. There is a fruit and vegetable stand, bedding plants, a snack bar, playground, and picnic area. Over the years, this railroad has grown. It is now one-third-mile long and plans are for more tracks and a larger gauge train.

Directions: Just a short distance down Holly Road from the turn off to the dahlia farm, heading toward the Canby Ferry.

Mollala River State Park
Canby
Hours: Closes at 8pm

This is a wonderful, under-used, state park. There are complete park/picnic facilities including a boat launch. Paved trails make the entire area accessible. Take the footbridge across the marsh to a cool grove of trees for a picnic. There are ducks, lots of frogs, turtles, and fish.

Directions: A short distance down the road from the Holly and Phoenix Railroad. Before the Canby Ferry, a sign for the park marks the entrance.

Canby Ferry $
Hours: Daily. 6:45am to 9pm

A wooden ferry began operation here in 1914. The present ferry is run by Clackamas County. The boat is named M.J. Lee, after the first pioneer child born in Canby. The ride takes about 5 minutes.

Directions: Follow signs to ferry. When you get to the other side of the Willamette River there are signs to direct you back to I-5, I-205 near the Stafford Road exit.

Hart's Reptile World $
11264 S. Mackburg Rd.
Canby, 266-7236

Ride Sherman, a 300-pound tortoise, visit Wilbur the croco-dile, and pet Penelope the python. There are more than 300 rep-tiles on display.

SAUVIE ISLAND

Sauvie Island is a little bit of tranquil country very close to Portland. It offers many opportunities for great activities with chil-dren. The island is known for its farms, beaches, wildlife areas, and cycling opportunities.

Sauvie Island is Oregon's largest island with 24,064 acres of lakes, beaches, farmland and river bottom habitat. The island is 15.1 miles long, 4.55 miles wide, and is near to the confluence of the Willamette and Columbia rivers. The island is a major nesting area for a large number of waterfowl. More than 300,000 ducks, geese, swans, heron, cranes, and an occasional bald eagle can be seen.

The island has a rich history. It was a major Indian population center with perhaps over 2,000 living here in small villages scat-tered over the island. Lewis and Clark camped on Sauvie Island. The first permanent white settlement was made in 1838 by the Hudson's Bay Company.
Directions: West on Hwy 30 out of Portland. Turn right at signs for Sauvie Island.

Bybee Howell House and Agricultural Museum
Sauvie Island, 232-1741, (Oregon Historical Society)
Hours: Wed Sun., 12-5 pm, June-Labor Day

The Bybee-Howell House was built in 1856 and has been restored and furnished for that period. Tours are scheduled regu-larly.

On the grounds of the homestead is an orchard with 100-year old trees that is almost a "living museum" in itself. There are many unusual varieties of apples once grown in the Oregon Territory but no longer available.

The Children's Agricultural Museum is a collection of over 300 tools used for farming between 1840 and the 1920s, when gas powered machines changed life on the farm. There are films and photographs showing farm scenes from various periods. Children can climb on and touch some of the larger pieces of equipment.

An old-fashioned 4th of July celebration and the "Wintering In" during the last weekend in September are popular annual events. (see CALENDAR).

Directions: Hwy. 30 to Sauvie Island. After bridge, turn left.

Walton Beach

A two mile stretch of beach along the Columbia River.
Directions: Turn left off bridge and take Sauvie Island Road to Reeder Road. Follow Reeder Road almost to the end. The parking area is across the road from the beach. Cross the dike to get to the beach. There are portable toilets in the summer months.

Farms

Sauvie Island is famous for its farm stands and u-pick opportunities. At certain times of the year, particularly Halloween, many of the farms have special events for families, including hay rides, petting zoos, and fields and fields of pumpkins.

COLUMBIA RIVER GORGE — OREGON SIDE

Columbia River Scenic Highway

The Columbia River Scenic Highway, a feat of engineering in its day, was blasted through basalt rock in 1917. It is now on the

National Register of Historic Places. The road takes you through lovely fern-draped glens to breathtaking viewpoints and past one of the greatest concentrations of waterfalls in the U.S. You can drive the route comfortably in several hours, or you can combine the drive with stops at some of the parks, hikes, or waterfalls mentioned below.

There are 3 exits for the Columbia Scenic Highway from I-84 East. If you're planning only to hike, you might want to skip some of the Scenic Highway and take the second or third Multnomah Falls exit.

The first exit to the Scenic Highway takes you through the small town of Troutdale. **Depot Park** is located by the Troutdale Police Station. A short trail from the park leads down to the Sandy River and ducks, always eager for a handout. The **Depot Museum** has memorabilia from the Union Pacific Railroad and is open most Sunday afternoons, 1-4.

As you leave Troutdale, the road passes through deep woods. Watch for the wrought iron dragon sculpture just a few miles out of town, on the right side of the road.

Crown Point has one of the most spectacular views in the Gorge. Bring your binoculars and be careful of your car doors on a windy day. **Vista House** at Crown Point was built in 1918 as a memorial to Oregon pioneers. It has interpretive displays, a viewing deck, and gift shop. Vista House is usually open by 10am.

As the road winds down from Crown Point, you begin the water fall section of the Scenic Highway. There are nine major waterfalls in less than a 10 mile section of the highway! Several of the falls are particularly good hikes for children. Most of the falls have picnic areas nearby, or are adjacent to state parks.

Latourelle Falls—short trail to falls

Wahkeena Falls—pleasant hike and particularly lovely picnic area

Multnomah Falls—spectacular falls, good hiking, bridges, and the restaurant has delicious cinnamon rolls, handicap access.

Horestail Falls—hike steep for very young children
Bridal Veil Falls—short hike to falls

Exit the Scenic Highway several miles past Horsetail Falls and return to Portland on I-84.

1-84 Points of Interest
These are just a few of many possible activities along I-84.

Rooster Rock State Park

Twenty two miles east of Portland. Big sandy beaches and good river swimming. Facilities for handicapped.

Benson State Park

Thirty miles east of Portland. Comfortable picnic area and swimming. Facilities for handicapped.

Elowha Falls Trail/McCord Creek

A good family hike. One mile to Upper Elowha Falls, and .8 mile to lower Elowha Falls.
Directions: I-84 east to exit 35, Ainsworth Park. Turn left at the end of exit, follow signs to Dodson and Warrendale. Travel east on Frontage Road for 2.3 miles. There is a parking area. Immediately after starting the hike you will see an old water tank.

Bonneville Dam/Bonneville Fish Hatchery

Bonneville Dam, built in 1937, was the first hydroelectric dam on the Columbia River. There is a lot to see here, with both the hatchery and the dam, so be sure to allow plenty of time. The grounds around the picnic area are well maintained and there are tables and a children's playground. The dam is 37 miles from Portland.

When coming into the area you will be able to go either to the dam and visitors center or turn left for the Fish Hatchery. If you're going to the dam, park either below and to the left of the big power station and locks, or drive up top near the visitors center.

To reach the navigation locks, climb the long stairway near the lower parking area. If you're lucky you can see a ship coming through the locks.

In addition to many informational displays, the visitors center provides underwater viewing of salmon and steelhead swimming up the fish ladders. Best viewing times are March -November.

There is another Bonneville Visitors Center located on the Washington side of the river. It can be reached by crossing the Bridge of the Gods in Hood River, and turning left on Highway 14.

Bonneville Fish Hatchery has been in operation since 1909. Don't miss it. You can see how the eggs are extracted, watch the feeding, and see the enormous sturgeon. There are 58 rearing ponds, 5 adult holding ponds, a factory for the egg extractions, and a fish ladder.

Cascade Locks Marine Park

Cascade Locks Marine Park has a large playground and picnic area on the Columbia River. At one end of the park is the Cascade Locks Historical Museum. (Open weekends in May; daily June-Sept.12-5pm.) What is left of the old Columbia River Locks is located here, as well as the "Oregon Pony," the first Northwest steam locomotive. At the other end of the park, you can watch wind surfers battle the famous winds of the Columbia Gorge. The sternwheeler "Columbia Gorge" operates out of Cascade Locks mid -June - September. (see RIDES) The Bridge of the Gods provides access to the Washington side of the river.
Directions: Forty -four miles east of Portland. Take the Cascade Locks exit and continue east through town. Entrance to the park is on the left.

Hood River

Sixty-two miles east of Portland, Hood River is one of the finest spots on this part of the Columbia River to watch the rapidly developing sport of windsurfing.

Port Marina Park

This is a good place to catch windsurfing in action. The park has swimming, beaches, and a picnic area. Hood River County Museum is located here, and it is the future homesite for the Hood River Tall Ships Museum. Stop by the visitors center for additional information about the Mid-Columbia area.

Panorama Point

Viewpoint for the Hood River Valley and Mt. Hood. Great place to visit in the Spring when the blossom are in bloom.
Directions: 1/4 mile south on Hwy 35, turn onto Eastside Rd. Continue for 2 1/2 miles. Watch for signs.

Blossom Festival

April (see CALENDAR). Many of the orchards around the area have special activities for families. Several have events in the late summer or fall. Write the Hood River Visitors Center for a calendar of events.

Columbia Gorge Hotel

Relive the elegant Twenties at the restored Columbia Gorge Hotel. The hotel is built above Wah-Gwin Falls. There is a spectacular view from the bluff overlooking the falls and the river. The grounds are large and well landscaped. Their country breakfast is famous.

COLUMBIA GORGE — WASHINGTON SIDE

The Washington side of the Columbia Gorge offers many opportunities for unique views of this natural wonder. Highway 14 out of Vancouver travels for the most part above river level, so vistas of the river and the Oregon landscape are spectacular. The road is windy and the traffic is often fast, making it occasionally difficult to pull over, though there are viewing pull-over places every few miles.

Pendleton Woolen Mills, Washougal (See TOURS)

Beacon Rock State Park

Beacon Rock has been a landmark for river travelers since it was named in 1805 by Capt. William Clark of the Lewis and Clark Expedition.

The hike up the 848 foot monolith is only for the stout of heart. The walkway is .9 mile from trailhead to rock top. There are pipe railings the entire way.

The surrounding park offers campsites, boat launches, and hiking.

Directions: I-5 north to Vancouver. Take State Highway 14 east for 35 miles or take I-84 to Bridge of the Gods. Cross to the Washington side, and turn left on to Highway 14.

MT. HOOD

Mt.Hood is an 11,235 ft. dormant volcano about 60 miles east of Portland. It is also a mecca for outdoor recreation. The winter months are dominated by skiing, both downhill and cross-country.

There are major downhill ski areas on the mountain, and many cross-country trails. There are even specific areas for sledding. In the summer, the mountain offers almost endless opportunities for hiking, camping, and even summer skiing.

A first stop in your explorations of Mt. Hood should be the Zigzag Ranger Station for maps, directions, and information. The Rangers can also recommend activities appropriate for families with children. The station is located on Hwy 26, the main route to the mountain, in Zigzag.

Hikes

Lost Creek Nature Trail

This is a perfect trail for anyone who wants to sample the Mt. Hood wilderness but is not physically up to the rigors of hiking. A paved walkway weaves through the woods, along a stream and past a beaver pond. There is even a spectacular view of Mt. Hood. The scenic picnic area has wheelchair accessible tables. An unpaved trail begins in the picnic area and winds back to the road.

Directions: Hwy.26 to Mt. Hood. At Zigzag turn left at Lolo Pass Road (18). Approximately 4 miles on Lolo Pass Road you'll see a sign for McNeil Campground and Ramona Falls. Continue approximately 1.5 miles to road 1825-111, then 1/8 mile further to Lost Creek picnic area.

Barlow Trail
Still Creek Campground

This is a short hike along the historic Barlow Trail, the trail used by pioneers to cross Mt. Hood and reach the Willamette Valley. The beginning of the hike can be confusing. Years ago this area was a popular vacation spot and there are foundations of old buildings. As you enter the campground look to the right for a sign that says "Barlow Trail". The sign is above eye level because this is a cross-country ski area in the winter. Take the left trail. It goes over the log bridge and through a small marshy area. Here you will be walking on wooden planks. The first 2 miles are gentle with lots of wild strawberries in season, making it a good hike for children. You can clearly see the deep ruts left by the wagon trains using the old Barlow Trail. This is not a loop trail.

Back in your car, follow the gravel road that goes from the back of Still Creek Campground. A short distance down the road, on the right, will be the Summit graves, a small pioneer cemetery.

Summit Meadows across the road offered feed for livestock and inspiration for weary pioneers in the 19th century. The wild flowers are abundant and beautiful.

Directions: Still Creek Campground is located between Government Camp and Trillium Lake on Hwy. 26.

Ramona Falls

Ramona Falls is probably one of the most popular hikes in the Mt. Hood Wilderness. The elevation climb is gentle and the round trip distance is 5.5 miles. With lots of stops and an easy pace, it is a good family hike. One leg of the loop, which is drier, follows a deep canyon formed by the Sandy River. The other leg goes through a wooded area where you can expect to see wild rhododendron and wild flowers along Ramona Creek. At mid-point is the beautiful 100 foot Ramona Falls.

Directions: Hwy.26 east. Eighteen miles east of Sandy, turn left at ZigZag onto Lolo Pass Road #18. Follow it 4 miles. Turn right at the sign for McNeil Campground and Ramona Falls. Go .6 mile, cross bridge and past entrance to the campground. Keep going straight, or bearing left, you will see a large parking area. It is possible to continue 1 1/2 miles down the unpaved spur road. There is another parking area near the beginning of the hike. Walk across the bridge and turn right. The trail is well marked and heavily used.

Frog Lake

Aptly named, there seem to be millions of frogs in Frog Lake! Plan to make several visits to follow the development of the frogs from eggs in June, to tadpoles, and finally frogs. There is also hiking and fishing.

Note: It is tempting to fill a bucket with these little creatures. Don't! Their life span is short away from their lake.

Directions: Hwy 26 past junction with Hwy 35. Watch for a small store on the left. The next left will have a sign for Frog Lake Campground. Park in day-use area.

Other Day Hikes

There are many other day hikes in the area. At the Zigzag Ranger Station ask for "Day Hikes on Mt. Hood" and "Day Hikes Around Timberline Lodge."

Alpine Slide $

The Alpine Slide at the time of publication is closed. Watch for this exciting attraction to reopen.

Winter Activities

To park your car on Mt. Hood from November to April 1st you must get a Sno-Park Permit. You can get permits at service stations on the mountain or ask in your local ski store for other locations.

Sledding $

Sledding on Mt. Hood is almost a childhood tradition in this area. Every child needs to experience that moment of anticipation at the top of a hill and exhilaration of speeding down the mountainside with the sting of flying snow against their cheeks. And what winter would be complete without the tingling of cold hands and feet, and the smells of wet wool mittens and hot chocolate?

Summit Ski area at Government Camp have developed sledding areas. They have rentals and firstaid personnel.

Skiing

Downhill $

More and more ski areas are working to attract families. As a result, there are now ski programs designed specifically for children as young as 3.

Skiwee—Timberline Lodge Ski School -231-5402

Powderhounds Ski School-646-4168

Mt. Hood Skibowl-272-3206

Mogul Busters Skibowl-254-7461

Mitey Mites (racers) Skibowl-222-2695, est. 6

Cross Country

White River—Take Hwy. 26 past turn off for highway 35. The area is marked with signs indicating White River Cross Country Ski Area. Parking is on the right. Trails on the right side of the road are groomed and flat. Trails across road are more challenging with more uphill sections.

Trillium Lake —Take Hwy. 26 past turn off to Timberline Lodge. Across from old Snow Bunny Lodge, parking on left. The trail starts with a short downhill and then levels off.

Timberline Lodge / Wy'East Day Lodge

Dedicated in 1937 by President Franklin Roosevelt, Timberline Lodge was built by depression-era federal agencies, the WPA and CCC. The beauty of the lodge is a tribute to local artists and craftsmen who worked with the materials of the area and whose designs were inspired by the mountain and its surroundings. Timberline is on the National Register of Historic Places.

Wy'East Day Lodge was designed as a day lodge for skiers and hikers. It also has handmade furnishings and features 1980s Northwest arts and crafts. Both Timberline and Wy'East are open year-round.

Children will enjoy the snow that can usually be found somewhere around the lodge until midsummer. There are short 2-mile day hikes around the lodge. In the winter, there are cross country ski trails, as well as the downhill runs. For the braver souls, during the summer, the Magic Mile Chairlift at Timberline should not be missed. The lift takes visitors further up the mountain for an absolutely spectacular view. It is a good idea to bring jackets, because it is cold on the ride up the lift and at the top .

Directions: Hwy.26 through Government Camp. Turn left at the sign for Timberline Lodge. It's approximately 6 miles up a scenic, windy road.

OTHER FAVORITES

Kah-Nee-Ta $
Warm Springs, 1-800-831-0100

Kah-Nee-Ta is a resort and hot springs owned and managed by the Confederated Tribes of Warm Springs. It advertises sun-shine "300 days a year". Located east of Mt. Hood,it is a favorite destination for rain-weary Portlanders, particularly in the spring and fall. Of special interest to the day-tripper is the huge swim-ming pool kept warm all year long by the famous hot mineral waters. Kah-Nee-Ta offers a range of accommodations and recre-ational activities, including native Indian dancing.

Directions: Kah-Nee-Ta is about 119 miles from Portland. Take Hwy.26 east. You will see a sign for Kah-Nee-Ta, turn left and you will drive for about 20 miles.

The Museum at Warm Springs $
Hwy 26, Warm Springs, 553-3331

Tribal artifacts and items that tell the story of the culture of the Confederated Tribes of Warm Springs: baskets, jewelry, strings of dentalia shells, bead works, clothing, tools.

Bagby Hot Springs

A soaking spot for the weary for more than 100 years, Bagby Hot Springs continues to be popular. The temperature of the 136 degree mineral water can be regulated by the amount of cold creek water added to the tubs. There are single and group tubs in a bathhouse and in the open air.

Directions: Hwy. 224 to Estacada. (You can get information and directions at the Estacada ranger station.) Continue on Hwy.224 for 25 miles. Just past Ripplebrook turn right on Forest Road 46. Go 4 miles, and turn right on Forest Road 63. Go another 4 miles and turn right on Forest Road 70. Continue for 6 miles. The trailhead and parking area are about 1/4 mile beyond Pegleg Campground on the left. The 1 1/2 mile hike is mostly level.

COAST

COAST TRIP 1

This is a loop trip that takes you out of Portland on Hwy 30 along the Columbia River to Westport where you will ride the ferry across the Columbia River to Puget Sound Island. From here you will drive across a bridge into the little rivertown of Cathlamet in Washington. Out of Cathlamet, take Hwy 4 following the Columbia River, into Longview, where you connect with I-5 south to Portland. Here are some places of interest to visit along the way.

Caples House Museum
Columbia City, 397-5390
Hours: Wed.- Sat.,11-5pm. Sun. 1-6pm.

Built in 1870, this was the residence of Dr. Charles Green Caples and his family until 1959. The museum is furnished with turn-of-the century pieces. See a display of some of Dr. Caples old medical instruments and be sure to visit the Children's Attic, full of old toys and dolls. There is a collection of miniature dolls representing the First Ladies of the US, dressed in their inaugural gowns.

Westport Ferry
Westport

This small town is where you catch the ferry to cross the Columbia River to Washington. If you've missed the ferry take time to visit the lovely King Salmon Lodge Bed and Breakfast located by the creek.

The ferry trip is short and leaves you on Puget Sound Island. Take a drive or carry your bikes to tour this island of dairy farms. Notice the different styles of barns. From here, drive over the bridge to Cathlamet.

Cathlamet/Longview

Cathlamet is a sleepy little river town with a quiet marina and some interesting turn-of-the century homes. Out of Cathlamet head east on Hwy 4, along the Washington side of the Columbia River, to Longview.

In Longview, stop off at Sacajawea Lake Park for a cool break. In R.A. Long Park, near the Civic Center, watch squirrels safely cross the street, above the flow of traffic, on their very own bridge. From Longview follow freeway signs to connect up with 1-5 south back to Portland.

COAST TRIP 2

ASTORIA AREA

Astoria, established by John Jacob Astor in 1811, was the first permanent white settlement on the Pacific Northwest Coast. Here are some places to visit in the Astoria area.

Astor/Astoria Column
Located in Astoria on Coxcomb Hill

This historical monument offers a spectacular view from Coxcomb Hill. The column, which stands 125 feet up, features a frieze work depicting important local historic events. You can take the 166 steps spiraling up the column to reach a panoramic view of the Columbia River, including the bar and coastline, the surrounding Coast Range and the countryside.

Directions: From HWY 30, turn on 16th/17th St. and follow signs.

Columbia River Maritime Museum
1792 Marine Dr. between 17th and 18th Street
Astoria, 325-2323
Hours: 9:30-5 daily, May 1-0ct 1. 9:30-5, Tues- Sun., Oct 1-May 1.

Relics from dozens of shipwrecks, nautical instruments, charts and paintings are housed in a wave-shaped structure that, at 37,000 sq.ft., is larger than a football field! There's a model ship collection ranging from a three-inch miniature vessel to a five-masted ship measuring over 10 feet. There are exhibits on whaling and sealing, as well the discovery and exploration of the Pacific NW. Moored nearby is the lightship "Columbia," the famous sentinel of the river entrance which sailed up and down the Columbia River for over 30 years.

Astoria Firefighter's Museum
2968 Marine Dr., 325-2203
Hours; Fri-Sun., 11-4pm., winter: 11-5pm., summer.

A collection of antique firefighting gear, some of it dating back to the 1880's. The museum is housed in a former fire hall. One piece of equipment, a Stutz pumper, was used to fight the great fire of Dec. 8, 1922, that destroyed 32 blocks of downtown Astoria.

Port of Astoria

After visiting the Museum, take a walk along the waterfront.

The Port of Astoria handles goods from all over the world. From higher points in the city you can get a better sense of this busy waterfront.

Astoria Bridge $

The Astoria Bridge was built in 1966 and is the longest continuous truss bridge in the world. Before the bridge was built ferries transported vehicles between Washington and Oregon.

Flavel House/ Clatsop County Museum
441 Eighth Street

Built in 1884 by Captain George Flavel, this house is considered one of the finest examples of Victorian architecture in Oregon. The inside is an interesting collection of Clatsop County history.

Fort Astoria
Exchange Street, between 14th and 15th St.
Astoria

Built by John Jacob Astor in 1811 to protect his fur trading company, Fort Astoria has been partially restored. Also nearby is the site of the first U.S.Post Office west of the Rocky Mountains, established in 1847.

Fort Clatsop
Off Hwy.101, between Astoria and Warrenton, 861-2471
Hours: Summer 8-6 daily. Winter 8-5 daily.

Named after the Indian tribe, this is a reconstruction of the fort that was built to shelter the Lewis and Clark party during the winter of 1805-06. During the summer, park rangers don period costumes and re-enact life at the fort. A wood chip path leads down to the fort's old canoe landing.

Directions: From Astoria, take US 101 south about four miles, turn left at the sign for the fort and follow signs about two miles.

Fort Stevens State Park
Southwest of Astoria
Hours: Summer. 10-6 daily. Winter. 8-4 Weekdays

Fort Stevens was built near the end of the Civil War to prevent the Confederate ships from sailing up the Columbia River and was later used for coast artillery. During WWII the Japanese fired on the fort, making it the only US military site on the continental United States to be attacked by an enemy since the War of 1812. Along the shoreline bordering the Park is the rusting hulk of the "Peter Iredale", a British ship which ran aground in 1906 .

The State Park includes picnicking/camping and seven miles of paved bike paths. There is excellent bird-watching near the estuaries and sand dunes.

Directions: From US 101 turn at the end of the Youngs Bay Bridge south of Astoria. Follow the signs to the park-about 8 miles.

Note: There are brochures at the visitors center for self-guided tours of the batteries and historic exhibits.

Fort Columbia
Off Hwy. 101, Washington
Hours: Open daily dawn-dusk
Interpretive Center open 9-5

Built in the early 1900's, the fort now houses an interpretive center, a small museum,a youth hostel, and an art gallery. There's a mile-long hiking trail through the area taking you through the batteries, gun turrets and underground bunkrooms. (Flashlights would be helpful.)

Directions from Astoria: Take the Astoria Bridge to Washington on US 101-head NW for approx two miles.

Fort Canby State Park
Ilwaco, Washington

A ten minute walk from Cape Disappointment Lighthouse is the Lewis and Clark Interpretive Center. Inside the center you'll find historic memorabilia from early fort and Coast Guard days. There is also a sail-powered lifesaving boat. There are two trailheads that end in spectacular ocean views and have places to picnic, fish, and swim.

Directions: From Astoria, take the bridge across to Washington, take US 101 and follow signs to Ilwaco. Watch the park signs for three miles.

COAST TRIP 3

SEASIDE-CANNON BEACH

The Seaside/ Cannon Beach area has been a popular vacation area and day trip destination for Portlanders for many years. Taking Hwy. 26 from Portland, the trip requires about and hour and a half, depending on traffic.

Jewel Wildlife Management
755-2264

From September through March one may see anywhere from 150-300 herd of Elk. Black Tail Deer and Eagles can also be spotted.

Directions: From Hwy 26 take Jewel/Mist exit, travel along Nehalem River approx. 9 miles, take Hwy 202 to Astoria, viewing is two miles up ahead.

Camp 18
Hwy 26 at milepost 18
755-1818
Hours: Daily 6am-9pm.

A museum of sorts, this rustic family style restaurant is decorated inside and outside with historical logging photographic, displays and equipment. Be sure to try the "Lumberjack Breakfast."

Seaside

The Seaside area was discovered by the Lewis and Clark Expedition in 1805. It was here the early explorers ended their journey. The numerous beaches are open and flat, great for the little ones. Seaside is a quiet resort area with several attractions that have special appeal to children.

The Promenade is a 6,000 foot long stretch of sidewalk built in 1920 that separates the beach from the town. This provides a great place to take a stroll, skate, or bicycle.

The turn-around at the end of Broadway Street marks the official end of the Lewis and Clark Trail. Broadway Street offers an assortment of giftshops, eateries and arcades. Two shops are all time favorites - Phillips Candies at 217 Broadway, famous for the saltwater taffy that has been shipped all over the US since 1897, and the Seaside Agate Shop at 408 Broadway, only a few agates but lots of toys, souvenirs, and one of the best miniatures selections in Oregon. A recent addition to the area is an antique Herschell carousel installed by members of the Portland Carousel Museum.

Lewis and Clark Salt Cairn

Members of the Lewis and Clark expedition operated a salt cairn in January and February of 1806. A reconstructed saltworks is maintained for public viewing on the site of the original. It is located on Lewis and Clark Way near the Promenade.

Seaside Aquarium $
200 N. Promenade

Hours: June-Sept.9-8:30 daily; Sept.May 9-5 closed Mon.and Tues.

This small aquarium offers a close look at sea life. You'll see crabs, an octopus that changes color, eels, a leopard shark and a sand shark. A special exhibit of frolicking harbor seals greet you at the entrance.

Seaside Museum $

Life in Oregon's oldest resort community is depicted through photographs and memorabilia. There are also exhibits on the area's logging history and North Coast Indians. The museum is open weekends and holidays.

Ecola State Park

Ecola State Park covers 1100 acres and contains over 6 miles of ocean beaches. Indian Beach is a popular surfing beach. There are several good hikes that offer grand views of the shoreline and the Tillamook Lighthouse. Deer and elk are numerous. Ecola Point is a popular picnic area and there is a paved trail out to edge of the cliff.

A small section of the Tillamook Head National Scenic trail is a popular walk. The hike begins about 1 1/2 miles after turning left at the tollbooth at the entry to Ecola Point. The road ends at Indian Point parking lot and the trail begins at the north end of the parking lot. At the fork in the trail turn left. After about 1/2 mile of climbing, you reach Indian Head and some spectacular views. Backtrack when you are tired.

Directions: Hwy 101. Take the 1st exit for Cannon Beach (north exit) and follow the signs for Ecola State Park. The road into the park is narrow and windy.

Cannon Beach

Twin Rocks, Oregon Coast

Named for cannons which washed ashore in 1846 as part of the shipwreck of the sloop US Shark, this coastal town is a growing arts and craft haven. In town, there are numerous shops and galleries. Cannon's seven mile beach area is dominated by Haystack Rock, a 235 foot monolith- one of the world's largest. Here are some of Oregon's most explored tidal pools. Located within a protected wildlife (sea life) refuge, one can discover and explore numerous inhabitants up close. Remember to look but don't touch.

At the north end of town, Ecola Creek runs into the ocean. The beach is protected here and children may enjoy the change from the ocean beach.

The popular "Sand Sculpture Contest" takes place in spring or early summer. Call for exact dates.

COAST TRIP 4

OSWALD WEST STATE PARK—TILLAMOOK AREA

Oswald West State Park

Oswald West State Park has well-maintained trails through an old-growth rainforest of massive spruce and cedar trees. The trails will take you to a picturesque cove. Avoid walking through campgrounds. Popular on weekends.
Directions: 10 miles south of Cannon Beach off Hwy 101

Neahkahnie Mountain Hike

Located within the Oregon Coast Trail, this five mile round-trip hike climbs to the 1631 foot summit of Neahkahnie Mountain. Legends from the 1700's tell of a shipwreck south of the mountain with the crew burying their treasure ashore in the side of the mountain. People have been looking for it ever since. Skeptics maintain that the mountain has shifted so much in the past 200 years or more that the treasure would be too deeply buried to ever be recovered. If you uncover any clues, be sure to write us immediately. The hike includes open meadows and forest on the way to a steep rocky meadow near the top. Near the summit, the trail becomes narrow and is very exposed, so watch your step and hold on to little ones.

Directions: From Oswald West go one mile S on US 101. Just before reaching the paved viewpoints, park on the wide graveled shoulder. Look for trailhead marker across the highway.

Nehalem Bay State Park

This state park extends the full length of the four mile Nehalem Bay spit. The park offers picnicking, overnight facilities, horse trails, and great bike trails for kids. It is also one of the few state parks that has an airport.

Directions: 2 1/2 miles off Hwy 101 at Bayshore Junction.

Nehalem Bay

Just south of Manzanita is Nehalem Bay one of Oregon's favorite crabbing areas. Here are a number of marinas where you can rent crabbing equipment and small boats to join in this popular excursion.

Garibaldi

The boat basin is located within Tillamook Bay, where Capt.Robert Gray first landed in 1788 mistakenly believing he was at the mouth of the Columbia River. Here you can walk the docks and pier to get a taste of the life of commercial fishing. There are fishing vessels of all sizes and designs, rigged differently for catching specific types of fish. You can also rent equipment for crabbing and fishing. Sign up for a deep-sea charter and try your luck. In March there is a "Blessing of the Fleet" festival.

The U.S. Coast Guard Station

A wonderful place to get an inside look into Coast Guard operations. You can board some of the ships. Peek into the control room and visit the boat repair shops and locker rooms. Guided tours are offered to the public after 3:00pm.
Directions: Off Hwy 101

Rockaway

101 Rock Shop
Hwy 101, Rockaway

You can't drive through Rockaway without stopping by the rock shop. Mr. Newcomb, the owner, knows all there is to know about treasures large and small. The shop is full of thousands of rocks/minerals from the local area and throughout the state, nation, and world. If you couldn't find that shiny agate along the coast you can buy beautiful polished ones here.

Newcomb also has shark teeth for a nickel! What a way to impress your friends back home.

Tillamook County Creamery/ Tillamook Cheese Factory
Hwy 101, Tillamook

A self-guided tour and a large screened slide shows visitors about the cheese-making process from start to finish. Large windows give you an opportunity to view the actual process. This plant produces over 25 million pounds of cheese a year. You may taste samples of the cheese and purchase it, along with other Oregon products at the creamery's gift shop.

Tillamook Pioneer Museum

2106 Second St., Tillamook

The Tillamook Pioneer museum contains a replica of a pioneer home and a great-grandmother's kitchen. There are also a number of collections, including old guns, pump organs, and Indian baskets.

Blimp Hanger Museum $
Port of Tillamook Bay, 400 Blimp Blvd., 842-1130
Hours: May-Oct., 10-6pm., daily

Located in the largest clear-span wood-truss building in the world, the museum houses photographs and memorabilia depicting the history of lighter-than-air (LTA) flight. There is a WWII barrage balloon, a hot-air balloon, and the Cyclo-Crane.

COAST TRIP 5

3 Cape Scenic Drive Loop

Three Cape Scenic Drive Loop, 20 miles in length, offers spectacular viewpoints, hiking trails, beach combing, natural attractions and a historic lighthouse. The scenic drive begins in Tillamook turn west off US 101 and follow signs marked "Three Capes Scenic Route". The loop travels by the Tillamook Bay area before climbing to Cape Meares State Park. Ten miles south, through Oceanside and Netarts, is Cape Lookout State Park. Further south you'll find endless sand dunes and Sand Lake. Next is Cape Kiwanda, the last cape on the scenic loop, and home of the dory fishing fleet. Continue through Pacific City and the scenic drive rejoins Hwy 101, 20 miles south of Tillamook.

Cape Meares State Park

On the way out to Cape Meares you will drive near Bay Ocean Peninsula. Stop and read the sign immediately to the left of the causeway for a brief history of the ill-fated Bay Ocean Park, that in

1910 was envisioned as a summer resort that would rival Atlantic City.

Cape Meares Lighthouse

This lighthouse was built in 1890. Thanks to its huge hand-ground lens it was visible 21 miles out to sea. It was one of only two eight-sided lights in America. The first light was provided by a flame from a kerosene lantern. A clockworks system of gears and weights kept the lens turning. The kerosene lamp was replaced by oil in 1910, electricity in 1934, and now there is an automated beacon near by. The historic landmark is open to the public during the summer months.

Octopus Tree

Not far from the lighthouse, within the Park, is an unusual Sitka spruce. The base of the tree measures more than ten feet in diameter with no central trunk. Limbs 3 to 5 feet thick branch out close to the ground much like the large tentacles of an octopus.

Cape Meares National Wildlife Refuge

This mainland refuge was established for protection of seabirds' nesting habitat. Of the 138 acres, most is covered by old forest growth. The trail in the park gives a close-up look at the vertical sea cliffs which drop several hundred feet. They provide nesting habitat for tufted puffins, pelagic cormorants, and pigeon guillemots. Binoculars are a must.

Three Arch Rocks National Wildlife Refuge
Off Hwy 101, near Oceanside

Viewing here is from the beach with binoculars. The Refuge was established in 1907, and the large rocks have long been the site of one of Oregon's largest seabird colonies. Over 75,000 winged creatures nest on every available ledge. There are tufted puffins, pigeon guillemots, storm-petrels, cormorants, and gulls. Sea lions are often visible on the lower rocks. At the north end of this tiny beach is a tunnel through the cliff to another beach creating a fun place for children to explore. Watch for hang-gliders when the wind is from the southwest or west.

Cape Lookout State Park
Off Hwy 101, 12 miles southwest of Tillamook

This park offers picnic and over-night facilities. There are numerous walking trails throughout the park either along the shoreline or into shady glens opening onto spectacular views of the coastline and cape.

Cape Lookout Hike

This hike can begin either within the park area or at the trailhead mark three miles past the park entrance. If you start at the trailhead mark, take the trail directly behind the sign. You continue straight ahead, descending gradually.

The cape is a prehistoric lava flow that protrudes 2 1/2 miles into the ocean. Along the trail plant and animal life are abundant. During April and November there's a good chance you'll see whales and sea lions. Near the end of the trail you'll hear the mournful sound of a fog horn on a nearby buoy, warning ships to stay clear of the rocks near shore.

Cape Kiwanda
Off Hwy 101 north of Pacific City.

Here you will find eight miles of rolling sand dunes and beach broken only by Cape Kiwanda. Hike up the dunes- this is not an area for those who don't like sand between their toes or in their shoes! If the wind is out of the west or north west watch for hang gliders launching off the cape and soaring along the coastline. If you want to catch the "dune buggy" bug you'll need to make a side trip to Sand Lake.

As you drop down on the south side of the Cape toward Pacific City, you can view the dory fishing fleet. In season,the fishermen/ women launch their 25-foot open boats, usually at dawn, by starting the motor on shore while the boats are still on the trailers. The trailers are then backed into the sea and the boats roar off. Stick around to catch the exciting return as the boat jumps from wave to wave at full speed, coming to rest high on the beach.

On your return to Tillamook through Pacific City to connect with Hwy 101, stop for a meal and enjoy the fresh catch of the day.

COAST TRIP 6

LINCOLN CITY AND NEWPORT AREA

Cascade Head — Nature Conservancy Trail

This two-mile hike (one way) travels though wooded terrain opening into a flowered meadow near the top. Here there are dramatic views of the Salmon River countryside, the ocean, and the resort area of Lincoln City. This land was saved from development in the mid-1960's by the efforts of concerned citizens, corporations, developers, and the Nature Conservancy. It now can be enjoyed by all.
Directions: Out of Neskowin head south on U.S. 101. Take Forest Service Road 1861 at the crest of the hill. Turn right and drive three miles to the trailhead. Look for the sign.

Lincoln City

Lacey's Doll House $
Lincoln City, 994-2392

One of the largest private collections in the western U.S.. There are over 3,000 dolls from antiques to modern Cabbage Patch Kids.
Directions: Hwy 101, Lincoln City

Alder House II Hours: 10am-5pm, daily, March 15-end of November.

Watch the 2,000 year old tradition of glass-blowing before a 2,000 degree furnace. " We'll blow it, hollow it, add more glass, block it, jade it, dent it, add bubbles and do all sorts of things to get the piece (glass) into the shape we want," says Buzz Williams, owner of the studio/shop.
Directions: Out of Lincoln City, near Gleneden Beach. Take Immoren Road off Hwy 101 (1/2 mile east).

Depoe Bay

Considered the world's smallest harbor (six square acres) Depoe Bay offers an exciting place to watch the pounding surf on a stormy day. Here one can safely enjoy the angry sea, spouting horns and sea geysers shooting through the jagged crevices and holes in the rocks below. Devils Punchbowl State Park several miles down the coast is another great place to watch the pounding surf. Be sure to hold on to little ones.

Newport

Oregon Coast Aquarium $
2820 SE Ferry Slip Rd., 867-3123
Hours: May 15-Oct. 15, 9-6pm., Oct. 16-May 14, 10-4:30pm., Closed Christmas Day

Watch tufted puffins call from 30-foot cliff tops and dive into a 9-foot deep pool, and walk through the largest open-air seabird aviary in North America. The $24-million facility is state-of-the-art. There is an underwater window that puts you nose-to-nose with sea lions, a rocky cave that is home to a giant Pacific octopus, and plantings of eel grass that hide tiny animals that live where a river meets the sea. Here you'll find rare sea otters, Leopard sharks, tidal pools, a play area for toddlers, a diaper-changing room, videos captioned for the hearing-impaired, some Braille materials and tactile exhibits, and the entire complex is wheel-chair-accessible.

Mark O. Hatfield Marine Science Center
Marine Center Drive, South Yaquina Bay, 867-0100
Hours: Winter 10- 4pm daily, except Christmas; summer 10-6 daily.

Here's the place to find the answers to all those questions you've had about the ocean and its inhabitants. A place for young and old. There are tours available or just wander through the center. There are exhibits of over 100 sea creatures, large informative murals, and a tidal pool to observe sea creatures up close. Stand beside the huge whale bone. Classes, workshops and trips for all ages are available year round.

While you are here you'll want to take a peek at the 180 foot "Wecoma", a research vessel manned by a crew of 13 with up to 16 researchers. The "Wecoma" functions not only as a research vessel but also as a college classroom for those enrolled in the college of Oceanography at Oregon State University.

Undersea Gardens $
Bay Boulevard, Newport ,265-2206

A visit here offers a close-up view of the kingdom beneath the sea. There are king salmon,an octopus and a moray eel, to name just a few.

The Wax Works $
Mariner Square on the bay front, Newport, 265-2206
This exhibit offers a slice of history as well as fantasy for the whole family. You'll not only see the traditional wax replicas of famous people from around the world, but there is also a realistic eruption of Mt. St. Helens, a sea battle of the past, and a space battle of the future.

Yaquina Bay Lighthouse
846 SW Government
Yaquina Bay State Park
Hours: Memorial-Labor Day, daily, 11-5pm; winter, weekends, noon-4pm.

Built in 1871, the Yaquina Bay Lighthouse is one of Oregon's oldest lighthouses, even though it was actually used for only three years. Saved from demolition and restored, the lighthouse and lighthouse keeper's residence is now a museum. Try to imagine the kind of life the lighthouse keeper and his family of eight children enjoyed in this tiny space!

Yaquina Head Outstanding Natural Area
Newport, 265-2863

Managed by the Bureau of Land Management, this 100-acre site (that includes the lighthouse) attracts more than 400,000 visitors each year. Wooden steps lead from the lighthouse area to fragile tidepools. Here, in a marine garden, you can view, but don't touch, such colorful, delicate creatures as sea anenomies, starfish, turban snails and sea urchins.

From a viewing platform west of the lighthouse you can see harbor seals through a spotting scope, and, with just a bit of luck, you will see the spouts of migrating whales. During spring and summer, a large seabird rookery is easily visable. Interpretive signs around the headland tell of the area's natural resources. A three-acre tidal zone is being developed at the tip of the headland that will be fully accessible to disabled persons.

When viewing the tidepools, we cannot stress enough the importance of tidepool etiquette. The taking, removing, or disturbing of marine creatures is prohibited.

ROADSIDE ATTRACTIONS

Woodstock Mystery Hole
SE Portland, 775-7909

A pitch-black underground chamber, origin unknown. Call to arrange a tour.

Abbey Museum
Mount Angel, 845-3030

The museum has an excellent collection of items willed to the abbey. See a giant preserved buffalo in a glass case; two, 8-legged calves; a stuffed Iguana and a porcupine; Samoan wood carvings; a collection of Eisenhower campaign memorabilia; slippers that monks once wore to mass and other liturgical artifacts.

Living Rock Studios
Brownsville, 466-5814

A museum made of stone and concrete and filled with paintings, carvings and sculptures depicting Bible scenes along with Oregon's natural history. There are thousands of rocks displayed in coffee jars, and a Tree of Life made of cement and petrified wood, surrounded by rocks.

White's Electronics Museum
Sweet Home, 367-2138

A one-room museum housing items found with metal detectors. The prize item is a wheel bully from a ship reportedly sunk in 1733.

Paul Jensen Artic Museum
Western Oregon State College
Monmouth, 838-8468
There are 3,000 artifacts gathered by Paul Jensen during his northern adventures, including a sod house, and a 27-foot Walrus-skin-boat, a gift from the natives of St. Lawrence Island.

RESOURCES

"50 Hiking Trails
Portland & Northwest Oregon"
Don and Roberta Lowe

"Touring the Columbia Gorge"
Pamphlet with points of interest on both Washington and Oregon sides of the Gorge. Available through visitors centers in Portland, Vancouver, Cascade Locks, and Hood River.-

"Best Choices on the Oregon Coast" William Faubion

"Oregon Coast Hikes" Paul Williams

"Oregon Free"
KiKi Caniff

"50 Old-Growth Hikes in the Willamette National Forest"
Found in bookstores and map outlets throughout Oregon.

METRO TRIVIA

Metro Trivia contains miscellaneous bits and pieces of information to titillate the imagination and curiosity of the young and old. We offer the following, sometimes unsubstantiated, trivia in the spirit of fun and challenge.

We welcome any additions or corrections you might wish to make to Metro Trivia. Please write us at Discovery Press, P.O. Box 80366, Portland, Oregon 97280.

• Portland Population — 430,000

• Portland Weather — Based on yearly averages

Portland's temperatures average a high of 62 degrees and a low of 44 degrees. We average 37 inches of rain year. There are 154 rainy days, 226 cloudy days, 67 sunny days and an average 2 days of snow a year.

• Back in 1845, Francis Pettygrove and Asa Lovejoy tossed an 1835 penny to decide what to name our city. Pettygrove won two out of the three tosses, naming our city after his home town, Portland, Maine. The loser was Boston.

• The first land claim in Portland was by William Johnson in 1842. He built a log cabin at what is now SW Curry and Macadam Street. A historical marker designates the almost inaccessible site. The marker is near SW Curry and Macadam, below the I-5 Freeway.

• The oldest house still standing is the Stephens house, built for James Stephens, who founded East Portland. The house, which is located at SE 12th Avenue and Stephens Street, was built in

1864. It no longer has its fine cupola and holds little of its past splendor.

• The first public building in Portland was a jail erected in 1851, by Colonel William King, near First and Oak. The oldest municipal building is the Pioneer Courthouse, still standing at Sixth and Morrison, built in 1875.

• The first school built from public taxes was at the present site of Pioneer Square at SW Fifth and Morrison. The school was dedicated on May 17,1858.

• In 1851 John Preston, the first Surveyor General of Oregon, placed "the starting stake" for all land surveys to be conducted in the Pacific Northwest. The stake, replaced by stone, is called the Willamette Stone. You'll find the historical marker off SW Skyline Boulevard just north of Burnside Street.

• Frank Beach is the man who nicknamed our city the "Rose City".

• Portland's bird is the Blue Heron. There are nesting and feeding spots in the city. For information on where and when you can see them, call the Audubon Society or the Portland Park Bureau

• The first paved street in Portland was at NW 26th Avenue and Thurman, and served as the entrance to the Lewis and Clark Exposition in 1905.

• To drive the curviest street, start at the intersection of SW Dosch, Patton, Humphrey and Talbot Roads. Take Talbot to Fairmont Boulevard (keep to your left at the intersections). Stay on Fairmont, making a circle back to the intersection where you started. This time continue on to Humphrey Boulevard to the Scholls Ferry Road intersection. From there take Hewitt Boulevard back to Patton and you'll end up once again at the intersection. You've just completed a gigantic figure eight! If you're not carsick by now there must be something wrong, so do it again!

• For the curviest drive in an enclosed area try the City Center Parking Garage, SW Fourth and Alder entrance (blue track side). Park at the top and when you leave you'll wind around and around in a corkscrew pattern until you reach the exit.

• The longest street in Portland is believed to be Burnside: It's over 20 miles. It runs from east county, through northeast, across the river and into southwest.

• The shortest street is SW Isabella off Vista - only 80 feet in length !

• The steepest street is SW College. Follow Hall Street to Upper Hall, to 16th Avenue. At College Street, turn east and head down to 12th Avenue. Be sure your brakes are working!

• The busiest streets in Portland are McLoughlin Boulevard with 40,000 trips per day; and Powell Boulevard with over 41,000 trips per day.

• The best sled ride in town, of course, is located near the steepest street. Begin at SW 16th, up near Elizabeth Street. Continue down 16th, turning right onto Upper Hall Street, and ending around 14th Avenue, near Portland State University. Most all of the cross streets dead-end. The traffic is light and slow — except for you !

• The Astoria Bridge is the largest continuous truss bridge in the world. The truss span is 1,232 feet in length and 4.12 miles long, connecting Oregon and Washington state.

• The Steel Bridge is the only bridge in the world where the lower deck can be raised and lowered independently of the upper deck.

• The Fremont Bridge has the fiercest winds.

• Four toots from bridge control tells a ship it can't come through.

• The Hawthorne Bridge is raised more than any other. The Hawthorne Bridge has a clearance of about 53 feet, and is up and down about 220 times a month. The Morrison and Burnside bridges, with 69-foot and 64-foot clearances go up and down just 12 to 15 times a month. The Broadway Bridge, which has a 90-foot clearance, is opened about 35 times a month, mostly for deep draft gain barges.

• The first Portland bridge over the Willamette River was the Morrison Bridge. The original one was built in 1887 out of wood. The Morrison Bridge is also the busiest bridge in the city.

• The skybridge joining Portland Veterans Medical Center and the Oregon Health Sciences University is the longest enclosed and air conditioned pedestrian bridge in the nation.

• Portland can boast of having both the largest and smallest city parks in the United States. The largest is Forest Park with over 4,700 acres, and the smallest is Mill Ends Park, 24 inches in diameter, at SW Front and Taylor. Portland's narrowest park is McCarthy Park at Swan Island.

• The tallest building is the First Interstate Bank at 1300 SW Fifth Ave. It is 546 feet from the sidewalk up. The US National Bank at SW Fifth and Burnside, is second at 436 feet 10 inches.

• Still the fastest ride in town (elevator ride) is located in the First Interstate Bank, 1300 SW Fifth. A sure way to make you turn green in seconds.

• Best outside elevator ride is found at the City Center Parking Garage, SW Fourth and Morrison.

• Portland has two castles! One is made of large stone, has a drawbridge and a moat. It is on SW Fairview, near Bennington.

The other is on SW Buckingham Street and is white. It can be seen in the hills as you drive south on Broadway, near Portland State University.

•The largest lake in the metropolitan area is Vancouver Lake located in the state of Washington.

• The highest spot in Portland is on top of Council Crest: elevation 1,074 feet above sea level.

• The lowest spot in Portland is the Delta Park area which is around 10 feet above sea level.

• Mill End store at 9701 SE McLoughlin, has the largest display of fabrics in the country.

• The downtown Portland's Saks Fifth Avenue is the only one of its stores outside Manhattan to actually be on Fifth Avenue.

• There are 2,623,834 screws in the Oregon Convention Center, about one for each Oregonian.

• The Lloyd Center roof has 40,000 square feet of glass.

• Powell's City of Books has the most volumes and the most square footage of any new and used bookstore in the country.

• Bruce Peterson holds the Columbia Gorge sailboard speed record at 42 mph.

• The Columbia Gorge's Wind River Nursery is the world's largest tree nursery.

• "The Spruce Goose" housed in McMinnville, at the Evergreen Air Venture Museum, is the largest aircraft in the world. It has a 320-foot wingspan, eight 28-cylinder engines--3,000 horsepower apiece, and is the only big plane ever made entirely from wood. It made one 1,000 yard flight and was never flown again. The museum is scheduled to open late, 1995. Call 768-5083.

• The oldest apple tree in the Northwest is off I-5 and Highway 14 in Old Apple Tree Park, Vancouver. (see DAY TRIPS, Vancouver)

• Portland is the Carousel Capital of the United States.

• Oregon City has the only municipal elevator in North America.

•Towers, tunnels and tires: The park with most playground structures is Greenway Park, Beaverton.

• The Willamette Meteorite, largest meteorite ever found in the United States was discovered by Ellis G. Hughes in 1902 at the SE intersection of Grapevine and Sweetbriar Roads in the hills above West Linn. The meteorite, which was 10 feet long, seven feet wide, and 4 feet high at the summit of the dome, had probably been embedded in the ground for over 10,000 years. A sign along Johnson Road in West Linn marks the historical spot.

• Portland's "weather eye in the sky" is a beacon light located on top of the Standard Plaza Building, 1100 SW Sixth Avenue in downtown Portland. It has provided Portlanders with an immediate weather forecast since 1963. White means colder, red means warmer, green is no change, blinking means precipitation and steady is no precipitation. A weather observer checks with the National Weather Service at least three times a day and changes the signal by a switch within the building.

• The largest ball of string in Portland, maybe Oregon, is located in the window of the Moller Barber College at 515 SW Third Avenue. The ball was started in 1922 from the string that came from the laundry bundles delivered to the college. There is over 50 miles of string wound into a 30 inch high sphere.

• The longest cape in Oregon is Cape Lookout.

Taking off from the Multnomah Hotel, 1912, Oregon Historical Society Photo

• The shortest river in the world is D-River which flows from Devils Lake into the ocean at Lincoln City.

• The longest picnic table in the world is located in the city park in Bellfountain, Oregon.

• The smallest harbor in the world is Depoe Bay, only six acres.

• The world's largest Sitka spruce tree is located off hwy 26 on the way to the coast. The circumference is 52'6", and the height is 216 ft. It is over 700 years old!

• One of the largest stone monoliths in the world is Haystack Rock, Cannon Beach.

• Beacon Rock is the second largest monolith in the world.

• Portland Area Bests
  Place to watch playground basketball—Irving Park
  Bowling Court (lawn)—Westmoreland Park
  Bird Watching—Oaks Bottom
  Skateboarding—Under Burnside Bridge, eastside.
  Bicycle Path—Tryon Creek State Park
  Stair climb—Contains 200 steps beginning on lower SW Broadway Drive and winds up to Hoffman Avenue. Called SW Elevator Street.
  Best star gazing spots—OMSI recommends that you can only get a relatively clean scan of the sky when you are 30-40 miles away from the city lights. Suggestions: Mt. Hood, Estacada, Larch Mountain, Bald Mountain, Vernonia, Banks and the Scenic Highway in the Columbia River Gorge.

CALENDAR

The Calendar is a month-by-month listing of some of the many events of special interest to families which occur each year at roughly the same time. The list is intended to alert you to watch the media or call for more up-to-date information on these events. Since there will likely be scheduling variations from year to year, we suggest that you check the Calendar a month or so ahead. We have tried to be as complete as possible, but if we have missed an event you feel should be included in future editions, please let us know.

There are many places such as OMSI that have continuously changing exhibits and will gladly provide you with their own schedules. (See RESOURCES section of this book.)

Good places to look for current activities for children and the specifics on the events listed below are:

Portland Parent Calendar
Portland Family Calendar
Oregonian, Friday's "Arts and Entertainment Section"
Willamette Week, "Fresh Weekly"
Downtowner

Abbreviations we have used:
WFC—World Forestry Center,4033 SW Canyon Road
MC—Memorial Coliseum, 1401 N Wheeler
MCEC—Multnomah County Expo Center, 2060 N Marine Drive

January

World's Toughest Rodeo—MC
Doll House and Miniature Show—MC
All Breed Dog Show—MCEC

Great American Train Show—MC
Auto Show—MC

February

Cat Fancier's Show—MC
Sportsman's Show—MCEC
Walt Disney's Magic Kingdom On Ice—MC
Portland Boat Show—MCEC
Lewis & Clark International Fair—Lewis & Clark College
Premium Horse Show—Clark County Fairgrounds

March

Northwest Food Fair—MC
St.Patrick's Day Parade—SW Broadway, Burnside to Main
Northwest Quilt Show—PSU, Smith Center Ballroom
Teddy Bear Clinic—Emanuel Hospital
Shrine Circus—MC

April

Trillium Festival—Tryon Creek State Park
Saturday Market Opening—Under the Burnside Bridge
Arbor Day—Plant A Tree!
Farm Animals & Easter Bunnies—Lloyd Center
Hawaiian Luau—Forest Grove, Pacific University
Hood River Valley Blossom Festival—Hood River
Easter Egg Hunts—Alpenrose Dairy, Oregon Humane Society,
Delta Park, Washington Park Zoo
Packy's Birthday Celebration—Washington Park Zoo
Toy & Doll Show—MC

May

World's Greatest Tricycle Race—Mt. Hood CC
Old Time Fiddlers' Contest—Clackamas CC

Imagination Celebration—Portland
St. Johns Parade Days—St. Johns Neighborhood
St. Helens Historic Days—St. Helens
Cinco De Mayo—Tom McCall/Waterfront Park
GI Joe Fish-In—Westmoreland Park
Children's Day—Japanese Gardens
Renaissance Faire—Lewis & Clark College
Children's Fair—MC
Lilac Week—Hulda Klager Gardens, Woodland, Wa.
Gay 90's Festival and Barbershop Quartet Competition—Forest Grove
International Children's Festival 1988—Vancouver, 206-695-3050
Fleet of Flowers—Depoe Bay
Sand Sculpture Festival—Cannon Beach
May Fete--White Salmon, WA.
Tygh Valley All Indian Rodeo
Kayak Rodeo--Clackamas River

June

Rose Festival Portland—A city-wide celebration
Starlight Parade
Jr. Rose Festival Parade
Festival of Bands
Grand Floral Parade
Rose Festival Festival Center
Ship Tours
Little Britches Rodeo
Hot Air Balloon Races
Post-Parade Float Display—Lloyd Center
Milk Carton Boat Races—Westmoreland Park
Queen selection and coronation
CART 200
Roce City of Roses Pow-Wow
Dragon Boat Races--Riverplace, Willamette River
Timber Festival—Molalla

Pickle Family Circus

Strawberry Festival—Forest Grove
Strawberry Festival—Wilsonville
Sesame Street Live—MC
Your Zoo and All That Jazz—Washington Park Zoo
Zoograss Bluegrass Concert—Washington Park Zoo
Cascade Runoff—downtown Portland
Hillsboro Happy Days—Hillsboro
Gymanfa Ganu Festival- (Welsh) — Bryn Seion Church, Beavercreek
Ft. Vancouver Days—Vancouver
Scandinavian Midsummer Festival—Astoria
Milwaukie Festival Days—Milwaukie
Strawberry Festival—Mt. Hood CC
Linn County Pioneer Picnic—Brownsville
High Wind Classic, sailboard races—Hood River

July

St. Paul Rodeo—St. Paul
Sandy Mountain Festival—Sandy
Molalla Buckaroo
All Breed Dog Show—MCEC
July 4th Parade—Hillsboro
Old Fashioned 4th of July Picnic—Bybee-Howell House, Sauvie Is.
Fireworks:
    Portland Civic Stadium
    Oaks Amusement Park
    Tom McCall Waterfront Park
    Ft. Vancouver—Vancouver
    Timber Park—Estacada
    Lake Oswego
    Sandy
    Washington Co. Fairgrounds—Hillsboro

Scottish Highland Games and Clan Gathering—David Douglas
High School
Neighborfair—Tom McCall Waterfront Park
Bluegrass Festival—Hillsboro

Concours d'elegance—Forest Grove
   (Vintage, antique and classic autos)
Estacada Timber Festival—Estacada
Multnomah County Fair
Wooden Boat Show—WFC
Chamber Music Northwest
Outdoor concerts in city parks—Portland Park Bureau
Living History Pageant—Champoeg State Park
Articipate—Portland
Music by Blue Lake—Blue Lake Park
Albany Timber Carnival
General Canby Days—Canby
Old Fashioned Festival—Newberg
Country Classic Horse Show and Festival — Inchinnan Farm,
   Wilsonville
Lake Oswego Festival of the Arts
Robin Hood Festival—Sherwood
Columbia County Fair
Cathedral Park Jazz Festival—Cathedral Park, Portland
Ft. Vancouver Fur Trapper Encampment
Columbia Gorge Pro-Am Speed Slalom (windsurfing)—Hood
   River
Salem Art Festival
Blue Grass Festival—Stevenson, WA
Columbia Gorge Pro-Am, sailboard races
Gorge Cities Blowout, sailboard races
Rosebud Relay—Portland

August

Washington County Fair
Clark County Fair
Clackamas County Fair
Aurora Jubilee and Folk Festival—Aurora
Tigard Town & Country Days—Cook Park, Tigard
Tualatin Crawfish Festival—Tualatin

Mt. Hood Jazz Festival—Mt. Hood CC
Bluegrass On The Mountain Concert—Timber Park, Estacada
Pickle Family Circus—Portland
Annual Antique Air Show—Evergreen Airport, Vancouver
Classic Music Concert—Washington Park
Oregon State Fair—Salem
World Music Festival—Portland
Blueberry Festival—Cornelius
Annual Corn Roast, S & S Farms, Forest Grove, 357-3006
Twilight Bed and P.J. Parade and River Bed Race—St. Helens
Astoria Regatta
Huckelberry Festival—White Salmon, WA

September

International Timber Festival—Estacada Timber Park
Autumnfest—Old Town, Portland
Artquake—Portland Oktoberfest—Holladay Park, Lloyd Center,
    Portland
Mt. Angel Oktoberfest—Mount Angel
Vancouver Sausage Festival—St. Joseph's School, Vancouver
Ringling Brothers Circus—Animals walk from NW Hoyt and 10th
    across Broadway Bridge to Coliseum before opening of show.
Wintering In Festival—Bybee Howell House

October

Annual Greek Holiday Festival — Holy Trinity Creek Orthodox
    Church
Portland Regional Gem & Mineral Show—MCEC
Bonsai Show—WFC/Japanese Gardens
Portland Miniature Show—MC
Portland International Livestock Show—MCEC
Helvetia Apple Festival—Helvetia
Children's Learning Fair—MC
Old Apple Tree Festival—Vancouver

Apple Cider Squeeze — John Inskeep Environmental Learning
    Center, Clackamas C.C.
Pumpkin Party—Washington Park Zoo
Haunted Houses—Check paper for locations

November

Verboort Kraut and Sausage Festival—Verboort
Baby and Family Fair—MC
Wooden Toy Display—WFC
Model Train Association, open to the public—288-7246
Peter Pan—Civic Theater
Doll and Teddy Bear Show—MCEC

December

Lighting of the Christmas Tree—Pioneer Square
Festival of Trees—MC
Meal with Santa—Meier & Frank
Santaland—Meier & Frank
Signing Santa—Jantzen Beach Center
Peacock Lane—39th and Peacock Lane, Portland (lights)
Nutcracker—Civic Auditorium
Storybook Lane Christmas—Alpenrose Dairy
Christmas Lights Parade of Ships on Columbia/Willamette Rivers
Sing Your Own Messiah—Civic Auditorium
International Christmas Tree Show—WFC Holiday
Woodcarving Show—WFC
Ethnic Christmas Display—WFC
All-Breed Cat Show—MCEC
Singing Christmas Tree—Civic Auditorium
All-Breed Bench Dog Show—MC
Christmas at the Pittock Mansion
Park Block Revels—South Park Blocks
Cut your own Christmas Tree—Portland Visitors Center for loca
    tions, or write: Northwest Christmas Tree Association, PO Box
    3366, Salem, Oregon, 97302. Tel. 364-2942

RESOURCES

We have included a list of some materials to help you continue your exploration of Portland and the metro area. For additional ideas see the RESOURCES listings at the end of some chapters.

PERIODICALS

"Portland Parent" $
P.O. Box 19864
Portland, 97280
721-4527

"Portland Family Calendar" $
1819 NW Everett, 220-0459

A monthly guide to what is going on of interest to children and families in the Portland and metro area. Also contains feature articles and regular columns.

"Oregonian" $
1320 SW Broadway, 221-8240

Daily newspaper, Friday's " Arts and Entertainment " section contains listings of special events.

"Willamette Week"
"Downtowner"

Free weekly publications with sections listing special events. Distributed on street corners and in neighborhood stores.

SOURCES

The following organizations are either good sources of information or have activities of specific interest to children and families. Many have their own catalogs as well as having their important events listed in other periodicals. If you want a complete list of activities, it is best to contact the organizations directly.

Visitors Bureaus

Visitors Bureaus should be a first stop in any exploration. You would be surprised at what you can learn about your own hometown. They provide great one-stop shopping for maps and brochures, which are usually free or at a nominal cost.

Portland Visitors and Convention Center
26 SW Salmon St., 222-2223

Vancouver/Clark County Visitors and Convention Bureau
303 E Evergreen, 206-696-8034

Salem Visitors and Convention Association
1313 Mill St. SE., 581-4325

Oregon Tri-City Chamber of Commerce
718 McLoughlin Blvd., Oregon City, 656-1619

Parks and Recreation

Call to get on the mailing list for published guides to hundreds of activities for all ages. Community centers and cultural centers may also have their own brochures.

Portland Bureau of Parks and Recreation
The Portland Building
1120 SW 5th, Room 502, 796-5193

"Discover Portland Parks"
Portland Parks and Recreation, 796-5193

Multnomah Art Center

Vancouver Parks and Recreation
1009 E McLoughlin Blvd.
Vancouver, 206-696-8236

Tualatin Hills Parks and Recreation
15707 SW Walker Rd.
Beaverton, 645-6433

Recreation Services for Disabled Citizens
426 NE 12th, 248-4328

Special Olympics
426 NE 12th, 230-1146

Outdoor Recreation
426 NE 12th, 230-4018

Schools and Libraries

Portland Community Schools
    Park Bureau,796-5123 or Portland Schools, 280-5780
Classes and activities located in neighborhood schools are spon-
sored by Portland Park Bureau and Portland Public Schools.
Schedules are sent to all Portland residents.

Multnomah County Library
801 SW 10th, Central Branch, 223-7201

Fort Vancouver Regional Library
1007 E Mill Plain Blvd., 289-1336

City of Beaverton Library
12500 SW Allen, 644-2197

Saturday Academy
Oregon Graduate Center

19600 NW Von Neumann Drive, 690-1190
Classes for highly motivated students grades 6 through 12.

Museums and Zoo

Children's Museum
3037 SW 2nd., 248-4587

OMSI
1945 SE Water Ave., 797-4000

Washington Park Zoo
4002 SW Canyon Rd., 226-1561

BOOKS

"Kids' Yellow Pages",Lois Shenker, Barbara Vanselow. Available local bookstores.

"Portland Guidebook", Linda Lampman, Julie Sterling. Available local bookstores.

"Oregon Free," Kiki Caniff. Available local bookstores.

INDEX

NOTES

NOTES

NOTES

NOTES